TURN YOUR
BLOOD, SWEAT
AND TEARS
INTO CASH

A GUIDE TO SELL
YOUR BUSINESS

October 25, 2017

James,

We enjoyed meeting you yesterday. Thanks for the wonderful tour. Hope to work with you soon.

E

EMERY ELLINGER III

Advance Praise for Turn Your Blood, Sweat & Tears into Cash

"With this book, Emery Ellinger positions himself clearly as the guy you want in your corner when it´s time to sell your business. He has parlayed his years of experience and expertise into a superb resource that is a must-read for anyone considering selling their business – successfully and for top dollar. A really terrific book".

Ernane Iung, Liquid Capital Corporation

"Easy, straightforward, enlightening read that any successful business owner will enjoy. It's not easy selling a business, I know this first hand. But, then again, neither is running a business… but with the proper knowledge and "blood, sweat and tears" it can be done and done profitably. This book clearly gives you, the reader, the knowledge (and confidence) needed to embark upon the sale of their company. Even if you have not thought about selling your business, this book is a great "business book" to add to your collection. If and when the day comes where you decide to sell your business (and you probably will), you will be glad to have this book in your library."

Ray "Raymow" Bradley, President,
Southern Landscaping Materials

"An outstanding resource to help guide business owners on how to maximize the value they receive for their company, while outlining the many challenges that most entrepreneurs face during their first business sale transaction. We experienced the Author's process first hand while selling our business and it delivered phenomenal results."

Keith Norder, Owner, Timberland Door

"Here is a brilliant and perceptive approach to selling your business. I was told by insurance companies and multiple hospitals that my primary care medical practice of 30 years had no cash value. I decided to contact Emery at Aberdeen Advisors. His team evaluated and marketed my practice and within a year successfully sold my business for a substantial amount of cash."

— George O. Brick, M.D., Owner, General Medicine Practice

TURN YOUR
BLOOD, SWEAT
AND TEARS
INTO CASH

I dedicate this book to all my past clients who have allowed me to shepherd them through the process of selling their businesses. Consequently, they won't be reading this book because they are off enjoying their retirement or other adventures.

Table of Contents

Book foreword by Bud Bradley

I met Emery through my son, who had a landscaping, irrigation, and pest control business. My son was actually looking to buy a company, but Emery mentioned to him that his business may have significant sale value because it was a hot industry at the time. My son ended up deciding to sell his business, so that he could move onto another industry that was of interest to him. He hired Emery, who did all the listing preparation work and had a buyer for him within a week.

I had been trying to sell my construction business for five years, with no luck. But seeing my son's experience with Emery I realized that I too needed to work with Emery. In that five years, we were partially in a recession, so I hadn't picked the best time to try and sell a business. That aside, the biggest problem I faced was that I didn't have any qualified buyers willing to pay me what my company was worth.

If I had access to the knowledge that Emery shares in this book about how to prepare my business for sale, I would have been able to sell my business much sooner than I did. I also would have realized that I shouldn't have tried to do it alone.

Prior to starting my business I worked with U.S. Steel for twenty years; during that time I acquired an MBA from Rider University in Trenton. I retired from the company in 1985 and immediately went on to found and operate a Tampa Bay area site utility company with my brother. In 1993, I left that business to create Raymow Construction Company. My business education served me well in organizing and operating multiple businesses. I was awarded contractor of the year in 2000 and 2006 by Suncoast Utility Contractor's Association, and inducted into their Hall of Fame in 2010.

All of my achievements led me to believe I could tackle anything—but selling a business was a lot more complex than I had imagined. Emery and his entire team at Aberdeen Advisors had the unique, niche knowledge that I lacked. They had experience selling businesses in my industry, and were very familiar with all the steps involved in completing a transaction such as ours. They got me results.

Emery's team was diligent and responsive. They put a lot of prospects in front of me and stayed incredibly well-connected with me on each available prospect. One of Aberdeen's team members was with my business team every time we first met a new prospect. It felt like I was their only client, because they devoted so much time and attention to my project. This is what you can expect from their high-achieving team.

Emery and his team understood that the sale of my business was more than a financial transaction for me. As a founder, it was part of who I am and they got me the deal I wanted under the conditions I wanted and the price I wanted. It was a win-win for all involved.

Turn Your Blood, Sweat & Tears into Cash: A Guide to Sell Your Business will help business owners properly prepare for the sale of their business, and overcome the problem of finding qualified buyers who can pay them what their company is worth. It will also guide you through some of the complexities of a business sale, saving you time and money, and earning you more money.

If you're like me, you may not even realize you need this help. But trust me, you do.

E.J. "Bud" Bradley, Founder/ Executive VP
Raymow Construction Company, Inc.
www.raymow.net

Acknowledgements

To my wife, Burchie, for her unwavering support on the roller coaster of building each of my businesses. And to my awesome kids, Burchie, Emery, and Crosby.

To my dad, who encouraged me to start my first business when I was 26 years old, even though I didn't feel prepared.

To Wendy Andrews-Fine, our VP, who has been key to helping build Aberdeen Advisors, and to the rest of the Aberdeen team for their support and collaboration.

And to Topher Morrison and Jodi McLean for inspiring my confidence to write this book.

Note to Readers

This book is for you if:

If you are interested in selling your business today, or within the next five years and:

- your business generates more than $5 million in annual revenues and is profitable
- you would like to better prepare for and understand the complexities of selling your business
- you want to learn what it takes to maximize the return for your blood, sweat, and tears

This book is also for you if you are an advisor or person of influence to someone who owns a business.

This book is not for you if:

- Your business revenue is less than $5 million.
- Your business is unprofitable.
- You are selling to a family member.

INTRODUCTION

You Are Going to Exit This Business, One Way or the Other

You've spent 10, 20, 30 years or more growing your business. You hired and trained a solid management team, developed a diverse customer base, and your company is generating over $5 million in revenues. You are proud of your accomplishments; you and your family are well aware of the blood, sweat, and tears that went into building what has become your legacy. The goal you had envisioned from the start has been realized...but you never envisioned how it would end.

It may have worked for you to pull 60-hour work weeks when you were younger; that's what it took to reach your goal, after all. Your wife supported your workaholic ways for many years—she may even have joined your team, helping out with the finances or such. But enough is enough, she has been telling you. She wants to travel and spend more time with the grandkids—and you do, too. But how do you get out of something you've grown to be so big? How will you continue to support your family if you retire? Who even *are* you, if you're not a business owner?

Though you may have been frugal even at the height of your business's success, have you really prepared for your retirement years? According to a 2016 statistic from The Business Insider, the average person between 56 to 61 years old has $17,000 in savings—likely not nearly enough to support your current lifestyle. Do you have a clear understanding of what your business is actually worth, and how to go about finding an ideal buyer? You have employees you want to be taken care of after you're gone; you have a comfortable personal lifestyle you don't want to change. How do you know when the best time to sell is? How do you know who the right person to sell to is?

These questions are on the minds of many of my clients. The truth is—very few business owners start with the end in mind. Their focus is on survival, and then growth, and more growth. Just like most people don't like to contemplate their own mortality, business owners don't like to contemplate the day they will no longer be in charge of their own business. But here's the hard truth—you are going to exit this business one way or the other. The real question is, are you going to exit in the way that is most responsible—that benefits you and your family and your employees in the best way possible? Or are you going to exit the business with no plan in place, leaving your long-built legacy to die along with you?

My role is to ensure that you choose the former. Even if you're not sure you're ready to sell just yet, now is the time to make sure you and your business are set up to earn the highest rate, undergo the smoothest process, and reap the greatest reward.

I'm not saying it's going to be easy—selling a business has become incredibly complex. I know, because I've been there—both as a business owner, and as an advisor. By the time I was in my mid-twenties, I'd built three direct-marketing companies, and sold them all successfully. But the learning process was painful. I was often intimidated and confused when terms like reps and warranties, indemnification, and reverse triangular merger were thrown across the negotiating table.

I had been under the impression that selling a business would be easy. In fact, in the last 10 years it has become harder to sell a business than ever before. Today, there is so much added litigation that needs to be managed—from human resources, to legal, to accounting. There are environmental liabilities, tax liabilities, insurance liabilities—all that if not handled properly, could affect the new buyer, and delay the sale far beyond what you had in mind. The increased risk to the buyer drives excessive due diligence on behalf of the seller. Likewise, there's significant risk the seller has to be careful to avoid.

Three Major Myths About Selling Your Business

Myth #1: "I will have no liability at closing."

Here's an example of an environmental problem in which the seller may be held responsible. Let's say you own a dry cleaning company; you sell your business and the property. Ten years later, there's oil found in the sand from when you owned the property, and it leaks into the water system. The buyer is going to come to you and say, "You didn't disclose this. You should have known. This was on you. "You're going to say, "You bought it. You had your chance to do due diligence."

There are going to be a lot of legal proceedings. Generally, in a situation like that, one of you could be responsible for $100 million worth of damage. Depending on the legal language used in the sale, this could be on you—even if you didn't know about the leak, and even if the environmental consultant you had at the time had told you that everything was fine. Talk about a buzz kill to the good life of retirement! If you don't have a lawyer involved with the sale, you could be on the hook for a number of liabilities. Don't let that happen to you.

Myth #2: "It's going to be easy to sell my business."

This one is a big fallacy. I have Baby Boomers come into my office and say, "Okay, I'm ready to sell my business. I want to sell it in three months" Let me tell you what, you're not getting a closing in three days. If you get lucky and find an ideal buyer within three days, they're not going to be ready to sign. They're going to come in and say to you, "I want to meet your key employees." Then they'll say, "I want to meet your key customers." Then they'll ask you for every customer contract and all the financials and all the insurance records—and they want them electronically. Many Baby Boomers—sellers now in their 60s or 70s—still have hard copies of everything. Today's buyers will REQUIRE all of your documents be in a digital format. As you will come to learn by reading this book, you need to prepare for the sale well in advance of your goal. And it's not going to be easy.

Myth #3: "I will get all cash."

Sellers also think their business is worth a lot more than it actually is, and that they're going to get all cash upon the sale. Of course they think it's worth more—it's their baby. They've invested the emotional sweat and often every last dollar of their profit back into the business. They know what it took to build their business, and no one is going to get away with what feels to them like theft. Often, their expectations need to be managed or corrected. Some sellers *do* get what they'd dreamed they'd get for their business, and some of them even get all cash—but it is more often the exception, than the rule.

You Don't Know What You Don't Know

It's impossible to be a subject matter expert in every field. Lawyers and CPA's and Merger and Acquisition (M&A) advisors are there to save you on taxes, to limit your liabilities, and to position your business for maximum value. We're going to help you get prepared so you know what to expect, and so you can get more money for the sale. We know you've been frugal—the sustainability of your business depended on it. But selling your business is one of those situations where you need to spend some money to make more out of a great deal.

You can try to do it yourself, but you're probably going to have fewer buyers. You are still running your business—you don't have the time to do it properly, and you don't have the expertise to achieve the results you want. Again, I know because I've been there. I learned the hard way, so that you don't have to.

Since I sold my first business, I have helped hundreds of people buy and sell companies in the southeast United States. Our Firm is consistently ranked #1 in Tampa Bay in sales volume in our market. I am incredibly passionate about what I do, because I see the difference our services make in people's lives. I watch our clients go from confused, unprepared, and misinformed to confident, relieved, and mainly overjoyed. They are grateful for their new-found freedom and proud of the legacy they have left behind.

I founded Aberdeen Advisors based on a vision to provide mid-market business owners superior results when they sell their businesses. We find the right buyers to help business owners get the highest sales price for their companies. I'm very passionate about the mid-market because when I sold my first mid-market company, I wish I'd had the support of a firm like Aberdeen. At Aberdeen, we focus on companies with revenues from $5 million to $100 million. We have structured our staff and managed our company to out-perform our competition on a consistent basis. We are committed to providing serious results for serious sellers. We do this in three ways: higher sales prices and stronger than average offers, unmatched closing rates, and faster closing times.

You may be surprised to know that only about 25% of businesses put on the market actually result in a closed sale. But at Aberdeen Advisors, our overall closing rate is 83%, and we have sold every single manufacturing client we've ever worked with. We deliver such consistent high performance because of our process. We know that finding just any buyer is not enough. We must find the ideal buyer to generate the best results—and in order to achieve that, we have to identify multiple ideal buyers. By finding these buyers, we are able to create competition for your business, which ultimately results in higher and better offers for you.

You may be thinking, "How much is my company worth? Who is likely to buy it? How long will it take to sell?" If you're serious about selling your company, keep reading. I will tell you everything you need to know to maximize cashing out and to turn your migraines into millions.

PART I:
PREPARING TO SELL

CHAPTER 1:
Why Sellers Get Stuck

You're a business owner. You either bought a business, or started one from nothing—either way, you've built it with your own blood, sweat, and tears. You've been through at least one recession, but somehow you made payroll. You've dealt with banks and lawyers and accountants. You've solved a wide array of problems—sometimes in the middle of the night. You've hired, you've fired, and through it all, you survived. Thrived, even—you managed to build a business that generates over $5 million in revenue. That's no small feat.

But throughout the seemingly never-ending, day-to-day decisions that you've had to make, did you make time to think about, well…how this was all going to end? Unfortunately, most business owners do not. Suddenly, 30 years have gone by and you realize, "Oh yeah, an exit plan. I remember how I was told to have one of those." It's like a business plan; you shouldn't start a business without one—not just in your head, but written down. Otherwise, you're 60 years old, thinking about retirement, and you're caught without one. You're trapped, but you don't yet know you're trapped.

I've seen it again and again. After *more than 15* years in this business, I have witnessed the above and the following all-too common pitfalls of selling a business.

Pitfalls of Selling a Business

One of the first things we do at Aberdeen when a client comes to us wanting to sell their business, is we look at their financials and show them what the business's value is. What most business owners will say is, "That's not enough," or, "I thought it was worth more." That's a common objection. What they think it's worth is not based on anything other than how much they've put into it themselves. That is the blood, sweat, and tears.

Nobody knows what you've put into this business as well as you. As much as you try to tell me, I'll never feel what you've been through. But at the end of the day, a buyer needs to make a return or they won't buy it—or they can't buy it because the bank won't lend them the money. While you may see the number and say, "This is only five or six years the income that the business is making now," the buyer is going to say, "I'm going to have to work eight years before I make one penny because I've got to pay the bank back. I've got to pay interest. I've got to get a return." Most people aren't going to work that many years without getting a return.

One of the common mistakes business owners make is believing that their business is worth more than it actually is…so they wait and they wait to sell, thinking they will find a buyer willing and able to pay what they think it's worth. But here's the problem: if it's a bull market and the $10 million value your business has now is not enough for you, so you wait to sell…all of a sudden the market will enter into a recession, at which time you may only get $6 million. If you are 62 years old and burnt out now, the more you wait, the less clients you will have, or the worse the market will be, or the worse your health will be—when you need to be on top of your game to close the best deal.

A general rule I've witnessed within this industry is that if a business owner gets to be 70 or 80 years old, they are going to go to the grave with their business. I got a call from a wife who told me her husband was dying; she wanted me to meet with her husband to determine a plan for selling the business. I met with the guy—who didn't know I knew he was dying— and I asked him, "What do you want to do once you sell the business?" He said, "I don't know. I don't golf, I don't travel. This is my hobby." I continued, "Do you know what your business is worth?" "I don't know, I don't know, I don't know." I drove away and called his wife. She asked, "Well, are you going to sell his business?" I had to tell her, "He's not going to sell the business. He's not motivated. This is what he loves."

What is sad about this situation, is that in this case he wasn't taking care of his family, employees, or customers. It sounded like the family needed the money, but he was going to go to his grave with the business—a business that couldn't be sold after his death, because he *was* the business. He'd had no exit plan.

I've had clients deteriorating fast in health; I said to them, "This business is tearing your health up. You need to go ahead and sell." They hem and they haw; they don't have clarity, but often their wives do. They tell their husbands, "Honey, you've got to sell the business." I had a client who had a $25 million trucking company; he died before he decided he was officially ready to sell. His wife tried to get in there and run the business, but it was closed within six months. It was a huge business, with big contracts. She just couldn't run it.

Another pitfall I see is that some business owners will hang on for ten years after they first wanted to sell, trying to sell to their kids. Often, the wives see that the kids don't want it—usually I can see within a minute if they don't. They may want to be the sales manager or the technical person, but they don't want to run it. I'm going to say the same thing the wives have been telling their husbands for 10 years, but if they hear it from someone that's not their wife, they might come around to the realization for themselves.

Most of the time I can spot sellers that are not ready to sell, but not always. I had a client that was 85 years old. He had the largest service company in the area. He could barely walk into our meeting. We met offsite at a restaurant; he brought his wife and his son. He said, "I am ready." I thought, "This guy can't even walk." I assumed he was going to be very motivated.

Well, he went to his deathbed with that business. I got him multiple offers; he said he didn't need the money, but he had $2 million in mind as his number. We got $900,000, $1 million, $1.2 million. When he declined the $1.2 million - given his profitability, that was really a high number - I realized, "This guy doesn't want to sell," even though he said he wanted to sell. His son wanted him to sell.

I'll have clients who are in probate and the wife will call. She'll say, "My husband died and we've closed the office. Can you sell the business?" I've had to tell her, "Well, if you closed the business, there's no business for me to sell. There's furniture. We don't sell furniture." I've had physicians' wives call me and want me to sell their deceased husband's patient list. I had to explain, that's not what we do—we sell ongoing, profitable businesses.

Another pitfall is the belief that, "Preparing to sell the business will distract me from the real work." Here's a wake-up call: Preparing for the sale *is* the "real" work. Sure, you have to keep your business going in the meantime—and going strong, so you're able to get a higher valuation for it when you are ready to sell. Selling a business is a lot of work, it's true. It can take six to twelve months to reach a deal. This is all the more reason to start early.

Don't wait until it's too late.

What is an M&A Firm?

As you've seen in the above examples, some sellers get stuck because they aren't getting offered the price for their business that they feel it is worth, they never commit to working out an exit plan, or they just don't *really* want to sell in the first place.

Other major reasons sellers get stuck include the following:

"My financials are a mess."

"I don't know what I'm doing."

These last two are where a Merger & Acquisition (M&A) advisory firm can help you. At Aberdeen, our advisors are used to working with a company's CFO, accountants, and auditors to clean up the Company's books and prepare them for entering the marketplace. Doing this first—and doing it well—will give both parties a clear understanding of the health of the business, and therefore a more accurate picture of the business's real value.

The M&A advisor is there on the seller's behalf. A great advisor will have a general range of knowledge regarding what companies sell for, and will have the skill set to communicate and negotiate with powerful buyers. Experienced advisors know how to properly prepare and present your business's financials so that they look the best when analyzed through the buyer's eyes. They will work with you to compose a strong teaser for the potential transaction, including both hard and soft value-adds. How these values are communicated to potential buyers can have a real impact on price and terms.

The expert M & A advisor possesses the knowledge and expertise necessary to showcase the many positive attributes of your company, to demonstrate the upside of your company, and to mitigate potentially challenging aspects of your company such as third party leases, customer or vendor concentrations, adverse safety records, or flimsy employment agreements.

At Aberdeen, our upfront collaborative approach with business owners has allowed us to prosper when it comes to successfully closing transactions. We possess the firsthand experience required to navigate through the complexities of selling your business.

As a business owner, you have likely negotiated hundreds of sales transactions, but I assure you the negotiation of the sale of a business, especially the sale of your own business, is very different. You're the expert at running your own business. An advisor should be an expert at helping you navigate the intricacies of the sale.

At Aberdeen, we dig into the details BEFORE we ever even market a company. We are very front-end driven in terms of analyzing your financials, identifying positive and potentially challenging aspects from a buyer's perspective, and creating marketing collateral that is professionally presented to select buyers. From the onset of the relationship, an advisor is there to facilitate the sale for you and to ensure a successful transition.

An experienced advisor will assist you with the creation of marketing materials, identification and vetting of buyers, preparation and completion of due diligence, and everything in between. The advisor will work in tandem with your team of professionals which should include your CPA and an M&A transaction attorney to ensure a successful transaction. While you're continuing to run your business, the advisor is marketing your firm, having multiple conversations with buyers, gathering additional data requested by serious buyers, and negotiating to get you the highest purchase price, with the best terms and conditions, per your expectation.

Additionally, a trusted M&A advisor doesn't leave you at the closing table; he continues to be available to you, post transaction through the integration process and beyond. For instance, there are many times when sellers do not get paid the entire purchase price up front. The transaction may include a note payable, an earn-out, or a true-up. The seller may retain stock. At Aberdeen, we sometimes stay in touch with our sellers for many years. Conversely, there are often times when our sellers get paid 100% cash at closing. When this glorious event takes place, the seller may decide to go to the mountains in North Carolina, the beaches in the Bahamas, or the Eiffel Tower in Paris! We don't generally ever hear from them again, as we achieved what they wanted, which was freedom.

How are M&A Firms Different from Business Brokers?

Business brokers are different from M&A advisory firms in many ways. For instance, business brokers generally lack the experience to sell at the level of capital that M&A advisors do. The average transaction size for a business broker is less than $250,000 while the average size transaction for an M&A advisor is much greater. Traditionally, business brokers have been real estate professionals who may also sell more main street types of businesses such as nail salons, gas stations, restaurants, or retail shops. Valuations for deals of this size are typically straightforward and the transactions have simple terms and conditions. The process normally involves a single buyer candidate, found locally. For the most part, business brokers passively market their listings with broad advertising tactics like ads, websites, and broadcast emails.

In contrast, M&A advisors represent larger firms with $5 million to $100 million in annual revenue. These deals involve higher sophistication and complexity, such as multiple locations, custom terms and financing options. And, M&A advisors market proactively on a very confidential basis to find multiple ideal prospects. M&A advisors have the experience to facilitate complex negotiations, properly prepare sellers for meticulous buy-side due diligence, and ultimately, successfully close transactions for the maximum value.

At a high level, the diagram below compares business brokers, M&A advisors, and investment bankers.

WHAT IS THE MID-MARKET?

Comprehensive M&A Services for the Mid-Market

Business Brokers	Aberdeen advisors	Investment Bankers
• Small, Simple Deals* • Minimal Support • Passive Marketing	• Success Fee Only • Full M&A Services • High Confidentiality • Active Marketing	• High Retainer Fees • No Guarantees • Handoff to Junior Team
*Average Deal $230k		

$5M ←————————————→ $100M

Serious Results for Serious Sellers.

How M&A Firms Overcome the Top Three Seller Problems

The sales process is daunting and presents many challenges. By partnering with an experienced M&A firm such as Aberdeen Advisors, sellers are able to overcome the challenges posed while advancing towards a successful sale.

In my experience, the three primary obstacles to selling your business are as follows:

1) **Limited connection to potential, qualified buyers**
2) **Lack of experience to negotiate a complex transaction**
3) **Limited time to run a successful sales process**

The primary challenge sellers realize when they come to me is that they don't know or have access to enough qualified buyers. Although "qualified" may encompass a myriad of things to different sellers, I am referring to the ability to secure and pay the amount of money that a company is worth. Business owners may know people who have expressed the desire to buy their businesses, but those prospective buyers may not be willing to pay what the business is worth or further, may not have access to the money to do so.

The second biggest challenge facing business owners ready to sell is that they do not have the experience or expertise to negotiate a complex business sale. When you are ready to sell, you will want to entrust an advisor that has successfully negotiated hundreds of transactions. You will want to engage a firm that has a proven track record with the complexities associated with a sale.

The third biggest challenge is that, as a business owner running a successful business, there is no time to effectively market, negotiate and handle the due diligence required to sell a business. When most sellers engage with Aberdeen Advisors, their expectation is that we will "just" find a buyer for their business. When the transaction is complete, business owners realize the enormity of the process and the monumental feat of getting from the initial launch of the business sale to the actual closing of the sales transaction.

At Aberdeen, we work fastidiously to assist sellers in overcoming these challenges with our six-step methodology for selling a business. Our proven methodology generates higher sales prices, unmatched closing rates, and faster closing times. Our process identifies and targets multiple ideal buyers, which transcends into multiple offers, ultimately resulting in more money for sellers, better terms and conditions, and a faster time to closing. Further, our process affords sellers more confidence and more certainty of closing because we rely on our experience and expertise to help select the BEST buyer based on seller needs and expectations.

Our six-step methodology will be outlined in Part II of this book, but here's a quick example of a deal we managed for a client using our six-step system: Strategize, Position, Market, Negotiate, Due Diligence, and Close.

An Aberdeen Success Story

I was hired by a seller who wanted to not only get top dollar for his business, but who also wanted to find the right buyer that would keep his legacy intact. Many of the strategic buyers he'd initially approached were competitors who wanted to change the name of his business and make it look like their business—using the same logo and so forth. What our seller needed was a high net-worth individual who was going to love his business like he did; someone that could see the value that had already been built and who just wanted to continue growing the legacy.

Our firm was able to find an individual that would let the seller still be the figurehead after the sale—who would not change the name, the logo, the address, or the people. We hand-picked this buyer, negotiated the economic terms that the seller wanted, took care of the necessary due diligence and positioned it so the seller would stay on for a couple of years to help run the business and transition it.

Our seller could not have achieved that result by himself; he was busy running a big business. He didn't have the time to market the business the way it needed to be marketed in order to find this buyer, nor would he have known how to position his business as a leader in the industry, so that he could get top dollar for it.

We achieve results like the above example all of the time. We know that the business owners that are going to win when it comes to the sale are the ones that have a manage-ment team in place, up-to-date, easily accessible, electronic records, financial reports maintained with integrity, and a proper exit plan. It's the people that come in and say, "I've got a top law firm, a top CPA firm, I'm with a top consulting or CEO peer group, and here's our five-year business plan," that are going to be successful. If you come and tell me those things, I can tell you that your company is going to sell for some good money, because you've got your ducks in a row.

To set yourself up for a successful sale, it's imperative that you do the necessary advanced planning. You need to get your financials audited, get your management team and information system in place, put your IT in the Cloud, and outsource your payroll and human resources so it's all buttoned up. Demonstrate a diverse customer base and employee team—don't have three clients that make up 60% of your revenue. Don't have one employee that brings in 80% of the revenue. Have higher profit margins than the industry—15% or more profit. Be growing at 5-10%. Have competitive barriers to entry, and recurring revenue. All of this and more.

Sounds complex, right? That's why we're in business. Business owners often come to us seeking instant gratification, but I can tell you that the fastest I have ever sold a business was a month, and some can take years, given the dynamic. It's not a simple process. But you don't have to do it alone.

CHAPTER 2:

I Had Become a Prisoner to My Business

When I first got out of college, I worked at a commercial bank. After that, I went to work at Merrill Lynch, where I realized I was an entrepreneur at these billion-dollar global companies. I started a business doing direct marketing for American Express, Delta Airlines, and Wachovia credit cards. We had a humble beginning; I didn't know anything about direct marketing when I first started.

We were very fortunate to make it through that survival phase. I thought I was going to have a heart attack at age 26, because we owed $40,000 and only had $10,000 in receivables. I moved back in with my parents so I didn't have to take a salary out of the business. I built the business with partners from several people company to a company with over 200 employees and $7 million in revenue; we were one of the fastest-growing companies in the country at one point. Then I sold it. The business had been fun when we had 10 or 15 people; it felt like a small family. It became more lucrative at 200 people, but there was more to manage. When the alarm went off in the middle of the night at our fulfillment facility, my wife said, "You're a prisoner to this business." That really stuck with me. I realized that she was right. I had to sell.

I should have been better prepared. I had not written an exit plan. As a result, I did not talk to enough qualified buyers, and I did not get multiple offers. I left a lot of money on the table. If I had worked with an M&A firm like Aberdeen, I would have had multiple buyers—Aberdeen may look at 50 to 100 to 150 buyers. Having multiple ideal buyers creates a competitive situation, which drives up the value of your business; you'll get more money with better terms and conditions.

I did have a good law firm that specialized in M&A, and I did have a good CPA firm. It's important to know that your current accountant may not have the expertise for a complex business sale—expertise that could literally save you millions of dollars in taxes. M&A advisors can connect you with the right lawyer and the right tax accountant to help with allocation of purchase price; maybe you also need estate planning to set up a trust to reduce taxes. Despite working with a top lawyer and accountant, I still got really frustrated with the due diligence. An M&A advisor could have handled a lot of that extra work for me.

After the sale, I went on to buy three other direct marketing companies. The three businesses I had were: a call center that took phone calls for the Olympics and Delta Airlines. We also had a direct marketing agency, and a mailing and fulfillment center that sent stuff out to prospects and clients. They were three good-sized businesses, that all worked together. When it came time to sell those businesses, I not only had a highly skilled M&A law firm and M&A specialized accounting firm on my team, but I had multiple people who had acquired multiple businesses serving as advisors. I ended up successfully selling all three of those integrated businesses to the same company.

I stayed on for the transition in that case, and helped them acquire four more companies. I worked with investment bankers to raise capital, which was very interesting to me. I had the financial background because I had majored in Economics at Washington and Lee University in Virginia. I had a corporate banking background from when I worked at a commercial bank. And I had an investment banking background from Merrill Lynch. I was then an entrepreneur, selling each company and buying other entrepreneurs.

After I transitioned out of working for those three marketing companies, I joined an investment banking firm in Atlanta, raising capital and growing technology companies. And then I served as COO of a company and we raised $6mm, and bought 3 companies in 90 days.

From there, I got a call from a Fortune 500 COO who had invested in a company in St. Petersburg. I got his call out of the blue and he said, "Hey, I want you to take a look at this company in St. Petersburg." I told him I was too busy.

He called back about a month later and said, "This thing could be worth hundreds of millions of dollars. Why don't you take a look at it?" He laid out a sales pitch. I got on a plane from Atlanta and flew down to Tampa and looked at the company, which was a small, public company. I met with the 74-year-old CEO, and he tells me, "I'd love to turn things over to you." My role was to hire the team, raise the capital, and help take the company to NASDAQ.

I agreed to the role, grew the company for five years and then sold off all the assets. Then I said, "Hmm, okay. Now what am I going to do?" I'd moved my wife and my kids to St. Petersburg. I thought, "Well, I love mergers and acquisitions and investment banking," so I got back into that. I joined a group out of Dallas, which was the largest group of business brokers in the country.

I learned a lot about valuations and mergers and acquisitions from working with that group for two years. They had the systems, the legal documents, the bankers, etc. Then I realized that even though I belonged to this network of 450 people throughout the United states, we didn't actually do a lot of deals together. I was one of their largest producers in the United States, handling deals by myself.

On top of that, the group was doing business broker-ing, whereas I really wanted to sell bigger businesses, in the merger and acquisition space. That's when I decided to start my own company—Aberdeen Advisors.

Now, my Company sells companies worth millions and millions of dollars, doing much more complex, bigger deals. We're selling to private-equity groups, selling to strategic buyers, and getting a lot higher multiples than what a busi-ness broker would do. I have sold over 200 companies, and our firm is consistently ranked #1 in our market. We're con-sistently #1 in our market. We're in the third largest state in the country and we're one of the top five producers in the state and #1 in Tampa Bay.

I love the mergers and acquisitions business because it's a challenge. My wife says, "I don't know why you do what you do," because it really is a hard business. We work with ego-driven, Type-A customers that are used to calling the shots. It's hard for them to have me come in as their advisor, and tell them what to do. My job is to get people, egos, strat-egy, banking, and finance all to line up; it's a really difficult puzzle. The reward is helping my clients get a result that they likely couldn't get without us, almost in every case.

If you are ready to sell your business, I look forward to the possibility of helping you achieve outstanding closing results too. I'd love for you to become another one of Aber-deen's success stories.

CHAPTER 3:
How Ready Are You Personally?

My company is selective with who we choose to work with; if a business owner comes to us and isn't genuinely motivated to sell his company, we will all end up disappointed. An incredible amount of work goes into preparing for a sale, finding and negotiating with ideal buyers, and properly handling all the paperwork through the closing. At Aberdeen, we don't get paid unless you get paid—meaning we successfully close the sale.

If you don't have a crystal-clear picture of what you want your life to look like after the sale, you're not ready to sell. Our process starts with sitting down with potential clients. We ask, "Why do you want to sell?" in five different ways. The most common replies we get from clients we take on are:

"I want to travel with my wife."

"I want to visit the grandkids more often."

"I want to spend more time on the mission field."

As a business owner making the decision to sell your company, you need a clear picture of what you want your life to look like after you successfully sell the business. You should be able to answer with conviction. Once we determine you are seriously motivated to sell, we'll conduct a deep dive into your financials. We will offer you a high-level value range based on our calculations and the industry standard multiples. We may come back and say, "We think your business is worth 8 to 10 million dollars." If your reply is, "I would never sell it for that," then we say, "Okay, then you need to grow your business and we can talk again once you've gotten it a little bit bigger." We know that if a seller wants to get $20 million for a business that is currently valued at $10 million, that's going to take a while.

Imagine somebody 60 years old, who has operated his business the same way for 30 years, and I come in and say, "Okay, you're going to hire a CFO for $175,000 plus benefits." They're not going to do that; if they haven't done it in 30 years, they are not going to do it now. They aren't ready for our services. Or if I tell someone, "Get your financials audited," but he refuses to spend the money to do so, I know that he is not ready for my team.

We are in business to offer serious results for serious sellers. If a seller isn't willing to be reasonable about the value of his business, he isn't a serious seller. If we say a business is worth $10 million and a seller is convinced it's worth $20 million, we'll just say, "That's fantastic. It's your business. It's your decision. It's possible you could get $20 million, but very unlikely." We'll probably not take that client on. The clients we do take on typically say, "This is what you do, and if you say I'm likely to get 8 to 10 million dollars for this business, then okay."

My role is not to try to change people. If someone is really not ready to sell, there's no benefit for either party in working together. Investment bankers charge the big fee—usually $10,000 to $20,000 thousand per month, with $25,000 up front. And, if you don't sell the business, you still owe them the money. At Aberdeen, our M&A firm operates on a success-fee-based business model; if you don't sell in the end, you owe us nothing.

I'm in the M&A business because I thrive on matching great businesses with the right buyer. I'm going to get compensated when we successfully unite buyers and sellers, but moreover, I am driven by the thrill of the challenge and by the emotional reward received from playing a small role in helping someone secure a better future for themselves and for their family. Further, it is of the utmost importance to me to identify buyers which will be good stewards for the legacies our sellers have built.

For example, I had a meeting with a client and a potential buyer. The buyer was looking at his Blackberry the whole time; he eventually got up and left, and the seller looked at me and said, "Emery, you're going to be mad at me, but I would never sell my business to that guy." I asked him why and he said, "Because he looked at his Blackberry the whole time. He was not engaged, it was rude." I said, "I agree. I wouldn't *let* you sell to that guy."

He was totally shocked. I said, "We're going to find the right buyer for you. That wasn't him." And we did.

Motivation is Key

The success of a sale comes down to having an intrinsic motivation to sell. If you are looking for the heavens to open up and all the stars to align before you sell, you're not intrinsically motivated.

Aberdeen has a client who calls a couple of times per year and inquires about the condition of the market. We have another client who reaches out to see if we have identified what he considers is the perfect buyer for his company, who in his dream is from an exotic place, will pay all cash, and will pay ten times more than the company is worth. As you would deduce, neither of these clients is motivated to sell.

From a seller's perspective, they believe that the reason they're not selling is because they haven't had the right offer, but I've seen how unrealistic and unmotivated sellers can be presented the best possible offer and there's still something else holding them back. For instance, I met with a man who is quite wealthy; he lives in a beautiful estate home, owns a high-priced speedboat, an expensive plane, and several luxurious cars. He was offered $10 million for his business. He came back and said, "No, I want $11 million instead of $10 million." Believe me, $1 million is not going to make a difference to this guy. He doesn't need the money; he just isn't ready to sell his business.

When I train my teams, they ask, "What's going to determine if we sell the business?" I tell them it's 100% seller motivation. The whole key is to find out why a seller is motivated to sell. If a seller is motivated, we can generally get an acceptable offer and that seller will sell. If they are only half motivated to sell, they may not sell.

Job one in our business is to determine a prospective seller's level of motivation. Perhaps the foremost indicator for whether a seller is motivated is whether or not he or she has a plan for post closing. In order for a seller to demonstrate serious motivation, he must have clarity of what he envisions for his life post closing. If a seller says, "I'm going to the mission fields." Boom. "I've got grandkids." Boom. These guys are very clear on exactly what they want to do. I had a client who said, "I want to travel with my wife; my wife has sacrificed for me, it's time that I sacrificed for her. We're going to go enjoy life." We closed and he flew to Spain.

If a seller doesn't have a post-closing succession plan and comments, "I've been doing this for thirty years. What else am I going to do?" Chances are, they are not a motivated seller. I once had a lady come into my office crying who said, "I don't want to sell the business, but all of a sudden I woke up and I was old." Time had slipped right by her; that realization can be a key motivating force. If a similar situation has happened to you, you may come to the realization that you are personally ready to sell.

CHAPTER 4:

How Appropriate is the Market?

One thing is to be ready personally to sell—to be clear on your motivation. Another step is to know when it's a good time to sell, according to the market. As of early 2017, we're in the fourth longest bull market in modern day history. Bull markets tend to last around five or six years; we're now going into eight years.

If you've been in business for 10 or 20 or 30 years, you'll remember what it's like to go through a recession or two—and therefore you should recognize that now is a good time to be a seller. If you wait until the next recession, your business valuation is going to go down.

A Seller's Market

At press time, we are in a seller's market; we have ten buyers to every seller of a good-sized company. There are plenty of buyers out there. The challenge for an M&A firm like

Aberdeen is finding sellers who have reasonable expectations, that are motivated to sell their businesses. Did you catch that? The challenge is finding the sellers, not the buyers. That surprises many of our clients.

They come to me and ask, "Do you think you can sell this? Do you think there are people that will buy this?" I tell them, "Yes. I'm not saying it's going to be easy, because it is not going to be easy." Sometimes the situation is the seller needs to find a buyer that wants to buy a business headquartered in a very remote area that provides a unique product or service. There may not be a lot of buyers for those specific conditions. There may only be one buyer; it can become a challenge in certain cases.

Fortunately, at Aberdeen we already have a databank of buyers. We have databases of manufacturing buyers, medical buyers, HVAC buyers and so on. For each client, we identify a targeted list of potential buyers. According to a 2015 study by Pitchbook, there are more than 3,500 active private equity firms. Further, according to the same study, the number of private equity firms grew 143% from 2000 to 2014. At press time, our firm had just sponsored an event in Florida wherein more than 400 private equity firms were in attendance. Towards the end of the multi-day event, I met with a private equity group that had $2.5 billion in cash, which means that with bank financing, they can basically buy $1 trillion worth of companies at market value.

It's not always easy, but in this market, we will find a buyer if the seller is well-prepared and his expectations are reasonable. If you've been thinking about selling in another year or two or three—now is a good time to ask yourself, "Is it close enough?" I had a client who was offered $10 million for his business, but he held on because he wasn't quite ready to retire. He waited nine months and his highest offer was $4.5 million, because the market had gone down. He was in a cyclical construction business, meaning when the economy went down, his business was directly tied to the cycle.

On the other hand, I've had a lot of clients that were smart enough to say, "I'm close enough to retirement. This cycle isn't going to last forever. I need to get my financials audited and get ready to sell now." They'd seen what happens in a down cycle; they'd be laying people off.

It's impossible to predict the future, but there's a lot of excitement among business owners that the bull market could continue for a few more years. Regulations put in place by Obamacare have stymied growth in business; people don't want to hire 50 more employees, because it would jump their tax liability into a new category. With a new government administration in place and the anticipated repeal of Obamacare, business owners feel optimistic that some of the current regulations will be lifted and the economy will experience more growth.

But what if the bull market doesn't continue? Can you sell your business during a recession?

A Buyer's Market

After the recession hit the United States in 2008, I heard business owners ask over and over again, "Can I sell my business during the worst years of my company's history?" Many of these business owners had owned their businesses for 30 years or more; they had reached the age of retirement during a recession, and needed to sell.

During a recession, it is definitely a buyer's market, but the good news is that there are plenty of buyers and plenty of capital on the sidelines. In order to sell the business, however, the seller must be willing to sell at market price—or otherwise wait for better days. Many times, an owner really does not want to wait another year or two to sell.

Even if your company isn't having its best years, in order to position it for sale, the most important thing is to make sure it is still profitable and on a growth path. To maximize your business's value, you need to develop credible projections that illustrate that your company is growing and will continue to be more profitable as the economy continues to improve. Detailed, realistic projections help a new buyer see the potential as sales continue to grow, and it helps them get funding from banks for the acquisition.

One scenario in selling during a recession, is that a buyer may offer to buy the business based on the current market value of the business, and pay additional monies for future growth. This additional consideration is sometimes called an "earn out." The earn out can be a fair way to bridge the gap between the current market valuation of a business that is coming off its market lows, and the potential value of the business if it continues to improve. The seller gets full value if the earn out is structured correctly, and the buyer pays the fair amount for the business. If the business performs, the buyer pays more; if the business does not perform well, then he has not overpaid. Of course, this leads to pitfalls if the earn out is not properly defined, or the new buyer does not run the business well. Nevertheless, it is a potential way to bridge the gap in the valuation of a business. Good legal advice is needed in structuring this type of an agreement.

Many lawyers will advise you not to have an earn out, and I agree if at all possible. Nevertheless, the job of intermediaries is to get the seller full value, and if the business is growing, an earn out is a method to bridge the gap between what the buyer is willing to pay and the seller is willing to accept.

Earn outs come in many forms. Typical structures are based on percentage of profits, or percentage of sales. If the business grows, the seller may get an additional bonus or earn out after the first year. Earn outs can be multi-year payouts, too.

So yes, you can sell your business during or after some tough years, but it is best to have the company rebounding in sales and profits, to have credible projections in place, and to be prepared to discuss an earn out in order to get full value for your business.

Growing During a Recession

Let's say you've decided to wait out the recession and sell after the market has rebounded. That doesn't mean there isn't work to be done while you wait—there is actually a valuable opportunity right in front of you, if you choose to take advantage of it.

My dad told me when I was a kid, "There will be three times in your life that if you have cash, you will be able to make a lot of money." He was referring, of course, to "great" recessions. These create unbelievable opportunities to buy businesses, real estate, stocks and other assets at steeply discounted prices.

As a business owner, you have two choices: do nothing, or seize the opportunity.

During the 2008 recession, we helped several clients with bigger companies buy some of the smaller players in order to continue their growth. We helped:

1) **The largest Tampa Bay Commercial Lawn Care company, Raymow Enterprises, in the sale of its business**

to the largest lawn care company in the world, at that time, ValleyCrest.

2) A local dental company in the sale of its practice to a large dental buyer who was acquiring dental practices throughout the United States.

3) A local pest control company sell to a company that was buying up several small pest control companies.

In each case, the buyers bought companies within their industry to grow their sales and profits. If the market falls into a recession before you're ready to sell, consider buying additional businesses to boost your financials for when the market rebounds and it becomes a seller's market once again.

Could you expand into new territories, or add additional services? It may be cheaper to buy an existing company which already has those local client relationships. You may also want to buy a company that has an ancillary service to yours, and therefore be able to cross-sell those services immediately to your customer base. This means that you have increased the sales and profits through this acquisition, making it easier to pay for the acquisition.

Opportunity abounds for your business, whether the economy is in a bull market or a recession. You want to be ready to take advantage of what either situation offers.

CHAPTER 5:
How Ready is Your Business?

As we discussed in the introduction, whether you are ready to sell now or not, one way or another you will exit your business at some point in time. In an ideal world, you will have been preparing for that moment from day one, but if you're like most business owners, writing up an exit plan escaped you, as did the years leading to your retirement.

In the latter scenario, I recommend preparing your business for your exit between three to five years before you actually desire to put it on the market. To exit successfully, owners need the following three elements:

A Road Map

Exit planning is a process that helps you choose where you want to go as well as how to get there. Even if you had an exit plan from the beginning, chances are it needs to be updated, so do not skip this all-important step.

Experienced Guides

As much as you may have become accustomed to doing things on your own, it is critical you do not try to exit your business without consulting with a number of experts in this niche. You must assemble a team of trained and experienced advisors to guide you toward your unique exit goals as you continue to run your company.

Implementation

Success depends upon a disciplined implementation timetable keyed to your exit plan. Without advisors experienced in exit planning, a written exit plan and implementation timetable, the chances for a successful exit are slim.

Here are some considerations to keep in mind when preparing your business for your exit.

7 Deadliest Mistakes When Selling Your Business

1) Owner is the Key Employee

The number one deadliest mistake a business owner can make when trying to sell his business is being the key employee. The best way to add value to your business is to have a management team and staff that know your business, and want to stay on with the new buyer. A buyer's risk goes up considerably if the only key employee is the seller;

consequently, the buyer will generally offer less money and want an extended transition period with the seller.

Most business owners we work with at Aberdeen are the founders; they are really too key to their business. They try to tell the buyer, "Oh, you'll have no problem," but they are the ones who know all the key customers; the transactional relationship is with them. They know the business, they know the suppliers, and they're usually making all the critical decisions. This reduces what they can get for their business.

The problem was from the beginning; they didn't build their business to sell it, they built it for their lifestyle: "I want to make all the decisions. I want to be hands-on." If they had built their business in order to maximize it, they would have hired a team, audited their financials, and so forth.

I sometimes send sellers away and say, "Go systematize the business and then come back. You'll get more for it." Having a turnkey business is going to increase the value. The goal is to build a more scalable business. If you are the key employee and you retire, what is left of your business? What is the buyer actually getting out of the deal?

2) Being Unrealistic About the Price

The second deadliest mistake a business owner can make when selling his business is being unrealistic about its value. While it may be fine to ask a higher than normal price, most buyers will simply politely move on to the next business for sale if they believe the seller has unrealistic price expectations.

In the "information age," buyers can source all types of data within minutes. With key information in the buyer's hands, the seller is reducing his chance of success by asking for a price that is "out of the ballpark," and then not being willing to come off that price. The real key is to be more flexible, and understand that there are market multiples for your business. In today's tough credit markets, a seller should expect to offer some seller financing and a lower price to sell his business.

3) Not Being Prepared to Sell

The third deadliest mistake is not being prepared to sell the business. Most business owners have never sold a business and get overwhelmed with the process. Having accurate monthly financials with at least three years of tax returns is critical. Buyers will ask for breakdowns by customer and other segments so that they can accurately understand what is driving the business. To provide credibility and experience in the financial due diligence phase of selling a business, it is important to have a good CPA.

4) Selecting the Wrong Buyer

There are too many stories of owners not receiving their full payments because the buyer ran the business into the ground. Selecting a qualified buyer who has the necessary experience, management skills and financial strength to buy the business is vitally important.

Furthermore, as I have mentioned throughout this book, Aberdeen plays a key role in assisting our sellers with the selection of the BEST buyer. Identifying and targeting the financially-qualified buyers is but one component to the process. The intangible components and the psychology behind an owner's buyer choice are oftentimes as important as the financial and experience components. For example, we have sellers tell us all the time that they do not care who they sell to, so long as that buyer's money is "good."

Then, we have those sellers who are equally concerned with their legacy and moreover, that the culture of their company remains unchanged. This elusive aspect is subjective and difficult to assess, as it is based predominantly on individual perception. I may think a prospective seller is genuine and sincere in his statements and that he doesn't want to change anything, while the seller may have the feeling the buyer is bluffing in terms of not changing the culture. Ultimately, of course, the decision is up to the seller.

Of the Aberdeen closed deals that do not work out, the primary reason is because the buyer came in and got rid of key people in the company. For example, I had a buyer who was going to keep two of the three partners on board and transition the third partner out. However, he ended up getting rid of the other two, and guess what happened? They lost the key employee under them, and then they lost the key customers. It was too dramatic of a shift, too soon. From there, it was a quick downward spiral for the company.

5) Waiting Too Long to Sell

We've already discussed this one in previous chapters. This mistake really shows its ugly head during economic downturns. Baby Boomers on the brink of retirement before the 2008 recession probably never thought they would have to go through such a downturn right when they wanted to sell their business and retire. Any issue such as the business owners getting burnt out, the owner having health issues and/or the business losing a key customer can make a business become virtually unsellable or sellable at a much-reduced value.

6) Selling Your Business Without Professional Advice

This advice comes from an array of resources including CPAs, lawyers, business brokers, M&A firms, business coaches and others. Many business owners that do not have a well-planned exit strategy just close their business because they cannot find a buyer, or they leave a lot of money on the table when they sell. Third-party professionals can help business owners get more money, with fewer tax implications in many cases, yet only ten to twenty percent of business owners use a third party intermediary.

7) Negotiating with Just One Buyer

Competition between buyers will raise the purchase price. If you do not have several buyers, then your chances of receiving the highest and most money for your business is greatly reduced. According to a 2013 article in Growing Business, "Selling Your Business: Creating Competition Between Buyers," when there are multiple buyers deals have been made "where the initial bids have gone up by 35% by the time the final price has been agreed."

M&A Advisors play a significant role in helping to create competition for your business. You need an open and competitive marketplace for your business. If the buyer knows there are other seriously interested buyers, the buyer will be more willing to offer more money or better terms.

In summary, if the business owner plans his exit strategy, then he will receive the highest value for his hard-earned work. This planning takes outside help and effort, and the results can be very rewarding.

The Most Critical Element for a Successful Exit Plan

As mentioned above, the #1 deadliest mistake a business owner can make is having only one key employee. This means they've failed to implement the most critical element for a successful exit plan—transferable value. Transferable value is what a business is worth to a buyer, without its current owner.

To give you an example of why this step is so critical, consider the case of one of my clients—let's call him Rick. Rick came to me, wanting to sell his business. He made over $1,000,000 per year, and asked if I agreed that his business would likely sell for about five times that income, or $5,000,000.

I asked him to tell me more about his business and his role in it. Rick proceeded to tell me that he owned a consulting firm; his role was to secure the consulting engagements, while approximately twenty of his consultants performed the actual consulting. His company had consistent cash flow, great customers and qualified consultants. But when I asked Rick who would stay on after he left, he gave me a blank stare. He explained that his consultants were not employees, but independent contractors. He had no staff.

I explained to Rick that without him, there was no one to oversee projects or obtain clients. Without him, his business was worthless. It had no transferable value.

Transferable value is a critical component to have at any time—not just when prepping for a sale. If a business owner such as Rick died today, he would be leaving his family without any income. He would not be leaving the legacy he had worked so hard to build.

How Transferable Value is Determined

According to John Brown of Business Enterprise Institute, it is buyers, specifically Private Equity Groups (PEGs), who determine the value of a business—not the business owner. PEGs remain the gold standard of valuators because they buy companies based on their experience, competition with other experienced buyers, and a thorough examination of a potential acquisition.

Brown states that PEGs analyze nine elements—or "value drivers"—to determine a business's value.

Top Nine Value Drivers

1. Next-Level Management (team that remains without owner's presence)
2. Operating Systems Demonstrated to Increase Sustainability of Cash Flows
3. Diversified Customer Base
4. Proven Growth Strategy
5. Recurring Revenue That is Sustainable and Resistant to "Commoditization"
6. Good and Improving Cash Flow
7. Demonstrated Scalability
8. Competitive Advantage

9. Financial Foresight and Controls

The sooner business owners begin to improve their company's value drivers, the more they benefit. If you wait until you're "ready" to retire, chances are you won't have the passion and motivation to reap the results you could have, had you started before you burnt out.

Starting early will also give you time to initiate alternative growth strategies (i.e. replacing non-performing management). If you're concerned you won't have time to focus on implementing these new strategies, remember you can always delegate the tasks you find uninteresting or unpleasant to other staff members.

It is important to note that the key to obtaining the highest price for your business is far more dependent on finding the right buyer than the method of valuing the business. Some buyers will only pay for the financial worth of your business, for example, asset valuation, earnings multiple and cash-flow analysis. But strategic buyers might see value in things like your location, customer profiles, expense structure or operational methods.

Exit Planning Assessment Questionnaire, by the Business Enterprise Institute

To assess your exit preparedness, please indicate your level of agreement with the following statements using this rating system:

0 – N/A,

1 – Strongly agree,

2 – Somewhat agree,

3 – Neither agree nor disagree,

4 – Somewhat disagree,

5 – Strongly disagree.

1. I know when, how, and to whom I want to leave my business.

   0   1   2   3   4   5

2. I know how much money I'll need, on an annual basis, after I leave my company to live a comfortable post-business life.

   0   1   2   3   4   5

3. The current value of my company meets or exceeds the value I'll need to retire comfortably.

   0   1   2   3   4   5

4. I know what after-tax value I will need for my business to meet my financial objectives.

   0   1   2   3   4   5

5. My key employees are (a) incentivized to increase the value of my business; and (b) motivated to remain with the company through targeted compensation benefits.

   0   1   2   3   4   5

6. I have created a written, realistic growth strategy for my company that aligns with my Exit Plan.

0   1   2   3   4   5

7. I have taken steps (such as covenants not to compete for key people and restricted access to trade secrets) to protect my most valuable business assets.

0   1   2   3   4   5

8. I've taken all appropriate measures necessary to operate my business in the most tax-efficient way possible.

0   1   2   3   4   5

If you intend to transfer your company to a family member or employee, please skip to 13.

9. I've completed pre-sale due diligence and addressed all issues identified.

0   1   2   3   4   5

10. I've completed pre-sale tax planning to maximize the after-tax sale proceeds I will receive.

0   1   2   3   4   5

11. I know whether, and for how much, companies in my industry are selling.

0   1   2   3   4   5

12. I understand the nonfinancial characteristics that make my company valuable to a buyer.

0   1   2   3   4   5

Please continue at 17.

13. If they had sufficient resources, I'd prefer to transfer my business to family or key employees.

0   1   2   3   4   5

14. I know how to transfer my business to family, employees or co-owners for top dollar while paying the minimal amount of taxes.

0   1   2   3   4   5

15. My company is free from family succession concerns.

0   1   2   3   4   5

16. My successor owner has the skills and knowledge to participate as an owner of the business.

0   1   2   3   4   5

17. I have a written contingency plan for my business should something happen to me.

0   1   2   3   4   5

18. My contingency plan includes a mechanism to retain key employees.

0   1   2   3   4   5

19. My estate plan protects my family's wealth by ensuring that it receives the full value of my ownership should I not live to transfer it.

                              0   1   2   3   4   5

20. My estate plan includes strategies to allocate business cash flow and transfer business ownership (and any related real estate) to the persons I choose.

                              0   1   2   3   4   5

Looking for a more in depth way to measure the readiness of your business for a sale? We have a tool you can use to determine your "Sellability Score." Take the test, and you'll receive a rating from 1 to 100, with a breakdown of which areas of your business you need to improve. Visit our website at **www.aberdeenadvisors.com** to get your score.

CHAPTER 6:

Getting Your Financials & Documents in Order

As we begin this chapter, it is important to note that having your financial "house" in order is of paramount importance to ensuring you are able to 1) attract quality buyers to your company, 2) drive the value for your company, 3) successfully and as expeditiously as possible, complete due diligence, and 4) ultimately, close the transaction. There are many other reasons for having reliable and transparent financials, but let's talk more about these three critical reasons.

Attracting Quality Buyers

Ideal, sophisticated buyers review the current and historical financials of your company prior to making any determination of whether to seek more information. If your company's financials reflect that your firm is profitable, that is only an initial determining factor as to whether a buyer will seek further information about your company. The prospective

buyer will want to review past and current financials to identify trends such as significant revenue increases or decreases,
capital expenditures, dramatic changes in costs of goods
sold or operating expenses, and so on. Trust me, you want a
buyer to perform a detailed analysis as this shows the buyer
is serious, motivated, and sophisticated. These types of buyers recognize value drivers such as strong financials.

Driving Value

The integrity of your financial statements is a key value
driver for your company. Specifically, your profit and loss
statements and your balance sheets must be accurate and
reliable. The composition of your financials should follow
GAAP and preferably be overseen by an outside accounting
firm who generates reviewed or audited statements for your
company.

Additionally, your financial statements should be generated timely and on a monthly basis. Ideally, your financial
statements should be calculated on an accrual basis to allow
buyers to have a more accurate glimpse into your cash flow
by better analyzing your accounts receivable and your accounts payable, current liabilities, and long-term debt. The
sophisticated buyer will recognize the value in your having
trustworthy financials. This can ultimately save the buyer
(and you) money, in terms of having to outsource a full audit
or full quality of earnings prior to the sale.

Finally, as a business owner, you or someone on your staff needs to possess an intimate understanding of your financials. It is important to be able to articulate to buyers how your company recognizes revenue, records and tracks inventory, and accounts for various expenses.

Expediting Due Diligence

In our business, we often say "time kills deals." It is in your best interest to already have your financial house in order PRIOR to marketing your company, so that this process doesn't delay the closing once a buyer is identified. Further, it is better from a positioning standpoint for you and for us to already be aware of any potential issues. That way, we may bring them to the attention of the buyer at the appropriate time versus having a buyer discover those issues later. At a minimum, having the buyer discover those issues on his own can de-value the company's position and perhaps reduce the amount a buyer is willing to pay. At a maximum, it can actually terminate the transaction with a given buyer.

Several years ago, our firm had a client that had increased its annual revenues from approximately $6 million to over $40 million in a single year. Of course, this dramatic increase in revenue resulted in a monsoon of interested buyers, but it also meant those sophisticated buyers were digging into every detail of the company's financials to determine the integrity of the data. Unfortunately, the company was still generating financials and following the same very loose accounting principles it had been using when it was growing from zero to $6 million.

The fact that the company's cash-based financials were not generated on an accrual basis was only the first issue. As you might imagine, the buyer list for a company of that size included only the most astute of buyers. These buyers were required to analyze every single detail of the company's financial statements and tax returns. An intense quality of earnings was mandated by all of the buyers, some of which expected the seller to share the costs of such. However, prior to any quality of earnings being performed, the seller had to have their financial statements accurately presented on an accrual basis, and to also do so for the two years prior.

This step, in and of itself, took almost three weeks and cost upwards of $30,000. Once revised statements were generated, the quality of earnings, conducted by Ernst and Young, ensued. This process took another month to complete. Ultimately, the deal never closed as during the months and months that the seller was getting their financial house in order, the market took a nose dive and the buyer pulled out. The message: time kills deals, so make sure that your financial house is in order prior to going to market.

Closing the Transaction

Having solid, trustworthy financials isn't only important at the beginning of the sales process, but also post-closing.

Although your attorney should make sure that you are protected in the event that something goes awry post transaction (via the reps and warranties part of the purchase contract), to further protect yourself, you need to be confident that your financials are without err. You need assurance from your accounting experts that the financials you present during due diligence and in the marketing of your company are accurate and have integrity, especially if your company is allowed some discretion in the compiling of the financials.

For example, most construction companies and some other project-based type of businesses may prepare or have their financials prepared on a percentage of completion basis. Without going into too much detail as we are not CPAs, according to Investopedia, the cost or percentage of completion method, at a high level, is simply an accounting method in which revenues and expenses of long-term contracts are recognized annually as a percentage of work completed during a given year. Let's say that your company secured a $1 million project in totality, but at the end of a given month, you had only completed 10% of the project and had incurred 5% of expenses. Your monthly financials would reflect revenue and expenses for the same.

The subjectivity comes into play as you, your sales manager or operations manager, or someone on your team, determines the percentage of completion, whether it be 10% or 90%. Of course, it is assumed that if your company tracks revenue in such a manner, you also have checks and balances or indicators in place which aid you in the determination. This type of accounting method can be very tricky, and I cannot stress enough how important it is to make sure as much objectivity as possible is utilized when drafting financials using this methodology. A CPA is definitely in order if you are using the cost of completion method.

By using the services of an experienced CPA, well-versed in companies such as yours, you can save yourself a significant amount of money in the event you have to revert, post transaction, to prove that you did not, maliciously or otherwise, overstate revenues or understate expenses.

At our firm, with a quick analysis of a company's financials, we are able to provide business owners with a high-level range of value for their business. This range of value is NOT a comprehensive valuation, but an opinion of value designed to set realistic seller expectations in terms of sale price.

The range of value is calculated based on the industry multiples of EBITDA, or cash flow, devised from previous completed sales transactions, on a national average. The opinion of value our firm provides is simply a range and most definitely, there are industry transactions completed within your designated industry which may fall well above the estimated average range. Ultimately, the market will determine the value of your company in terms of sales price so we always caution sellers not to get too hung up on the range of value. The worksheet below is a worksheet demonstrating the basis of our range of value calculation.

Opinion of Value Worksheet - based on Financial Statements

	Prior Year	Current YTD	Anualized
Revenue	$	$	$
COGS	$	$	$
Gross Profit	$	$	$
Operating Expenses	$	$	$
Other Income/ Expenses	$	$	$
Gain/Loss (=) Sale Assets	$	$	$
Net Income	$	$	$
EBITDA Adjustments	$	$	$
Interest	$	$	$
Depreciation	$	$	$
Amortization	$	$	$
EBITDA	$	$	$
Valuation Range of (____) to (____) times EBITDA for (Chosen Period Above)			

Aberdeen
advisors

In addition to your company's credible financial statements, a key component to determining a company's true cash flow for a prospective buyer is identifying the owner's benefit(s). By owner's benefit, we are referring to any and all personal expenses recorded within the company's financial statements.

For example, the owner benefit calculation would include the officer or officers' salary and health insurance premiums, if recorded as an expense on the company's profit and loss statement. The owner benefit may also include automobiles, meals and entertainment, pension plan contributions, travel expenses, and so on in the event these owner expenses are recorded within the financial statements. The exercise of extrapolating the owner benefits from the profit and loss statement allows a buyer to review the cash flow of the business in terms of what he will have access to. The buyer may choose to utilize this "discretionary cash" a different way, in the event that he purchases the company.

It is very important to note that when analyzing cash flow and using a company's profit and loss statement as the basis for such, any officer withdrawals or distributions not expensed through the company's profit and loss statement may NOT be calculated into the owner benefit worksheet. Many sellers are misguided and are under the belief that if they write a check to themselves or remove cash from the business that this is an owner benefit. Of course, it is a benefit to owning the business, however if such a withdrawal is not recorded as an EXPENSE on the profit and loss statement, it cannot be included in the owner benefit calculation.

The below worksheet may be used to demonstrate some of the items considered as "owner benefits."

When dealing with prospective buyers, it is a good idea to pre-qualify them on a high-level basis. Most serious buyers are willing to entertain a basic qualification process. The

Aberdeen
advisors

SELLER'S DISCRETIONARY EARNINGS CALCULATION

Financial data for _____ months   From: _____   To: _____

	OWNER'S RECORDS	(Adjustments)	Reason for Adjustments	Adjusted Amount
GROSS SALES	$ _____	$ _____		$ _____
COST OF GOODS	$ _____	$ _____		$ _____
GROSS PROFIT	$ _____	$ _____		$ _____
			ADJUSTED GROSS PROFIT (ENTER BELOW)	$ _____

EXPENSES	OWNER'S RECORDS	(Adjustments)	Reason for Adjustments	Adjusted Expense
Accounting	$ _____	$ _____	_____	$ _____
Advertising	$ _____	$ _____	_____	$ _____
Amortization	$ _____	$ _____	_____	$ _____
Auto Expenses	$ _____	$ _____	_____	$ _____
Bad Debt	$ _____	$ _____	_____	$ _____
Bank Charges	$ _____	$ _____	_____	$ _____
Commissions	$ _____	$ _____	_____	$ _____
Contract Labor	$ _____	$ _____	_____	$ _____
Depreciation	$ _____	$ _____	_____	$ _____
Donations	$ _____	$ _____	_____	$ _____
Dues-Subscriptions	$ _____	$ _____	_____	$ _____
Employee Benefits	$ _____	$ _____	_____	$ _____
Insurance - Auto	$ _____	$ _____	_____	$ _____
Insurance - Business	$ _____	$ _____	_____	$ _____
Insurance - Health	$ _____	$ _____	_____	$ _____
Interest	$ _____	$ _____	_____	$ _____
Janitorial	$ _____	$ _____	_____	$ _____
Legal	$ _____	$ _____	_____	$ _____
Licenses	$ _____	$ _____	_____	$ _____
Office Supplies	$ _____	$ _____	_____	$ _____
Owner's Salary	$ _____	$ _____	_____	$ _____
Postage	$ _____	$ _____	_____	$ _____
Rent	$ _____	$ _____	_____	$ _____
Repairs & Maintenance	$ _____	$ _____	_____	$ _____
Salaries	$ _____	$ _____	_____	$ _____
Tax	$ _____	$ _____	_____	$ _____
Tax - Payroll	$ _____	$ _____	_____	$ _____
Telephone	$ _____	$ _____	_____	$ _____
Travel/Entertainment	$ _____	$ _____	_____	$ _____
Utilities	$ _____	$ _____	_____	$ _____
Miscellaneous				
_____	$ _____	$ _____	_____	$ _____
_____	$ _____	$ _____	_____	$ _____
			TOTAL ADJUSTED EXPENSES (ENTER BELOW)	$ _____

ADJUSTED GROSS PROFIT $ _____
MINUS TOTAL ADJUSTED EXPENSES $ _____
= TOTAL OWNER'S BENEFIT $ _____

The above set forth information has been secured from the Seller. **Aberdeen Advisors, Inc.** (***Broker***) in no way guarantees the accuracy of such information, nor does it warrant any assumptions as true and correct. The Seller agrees that this information and other documentation will be made available through ***Broker***, or from the Seller, upon the acceptance of an earnest money "Offer to Purchase." The Seller authorizes ***Broker*** to disclose this information to any Prospect or his broker, regardless of said broker's "Agency Status." A faxed copy of this document and any signatures, shall be construed as original.

I certify that the above is true and correct _____ Date _____
                                              Seller's Signature

more sophisticated and more serious buyer will likely have already undergone a preliminary financial screening with a lender, in the event that he will require financing in order to purchase a business. He may have a clear understanding of the amount a bank is willing to finance based on his credit score, available cash, and so on.

The buyer financial statement below, similar to what banks use, will provide a seller's M&A advisor with a glimpse of a prospective buyer's financial qualifications. Advisors are generally NOT in the business of forensically evaluating a buyer's financial status but do so rather on a conversation and completion of a basic financial statement (see below). Obviously, the integrity of the personal financial statement is directly tied to that of the individual prospective buyer.

When our firm engages with a seller, it is our practice to gather as much information on the front end as possible. Even if a lot of the information (i.e. insurance policies) may not be needed initially, eventually, all of the information we request will be utilized either to prepare the marketing collateral or satisfy a due diligence request.

Below is our firm's INITIAL checklist to provide you with an idea of the documents which will be requested from you in the event you decide to sell your company. Once the marketing of your company to prospective buyers begins, there will be additional requests.

Aberdeen
advisors

FINANCIAL STATEMENT
(This information will be held strictly CONFIDENTIAL.)

Name: _____ Date: _____

Address: _____

City: _____ State: _____ Zip: _____ Phone: _____

ASSETS

Cash on Hand in Banks:	$_____
U.S. Government Securities:	$_____
Accounts, Loans, and Notes Receivable:	$_____
Cash Value of Life Insurance:	$_____
Value of Businesses Owned:	$_____
Other Stocks and Bonds:	$_____
Real Estate:	$_____
Automobiles – (Indicate Quantity):	$_____
Household Furnishings, Etc:	$_____
Other Assets (Itemized as Follows): _____	$_____
_____	$_____

TOTAL ASSETS: $_____

LIABILITIES

Notes Payable:	$_____
Liens on Real Estate:	$_____
Other Liabilities (Itemized as Follows): _____	$_____
_____	$_____

TOTAL LIABILITIES: $_____

NET WORTH = TOTAL ASSETS MINUS TOTAL LIABILITIES: $_____

SOURCE OF INCOME

Salary:	$_____
Dividends and Interest:	$_____
Bonus/Commissions:	$_____
Real Estate Income:	$_____
Other Income:	$_____

TOTAL INCOME: $_____

It is understood that this information will be held in strict confidence by Aberdeen Advisors, Inc. and its agents and officers. **The undersigned certifies that this information is true and correct.**

Signature: _____ Date: _____

CHECKLIST OF LISTING ITEMS:
DOCUMENTS NEEDED

____ Profit and loss statements and balance sheets for the last three years.

____ Latest interim financial statements.

____ Corporate tax return, Schedule C, or Partnership tax return for at least two years.

____ List of assets to be included in the sale.

____ List of assets to be excluded from the sale.

____ Schedule of all indebtedness of the business.

____ Copies of any patents, copyrights, trademarks, or contracts of value.

____ Legal description of any real property included in the sale.

____ Any employment contracts, representative agreements, etc.

____ Organizational chart (job description and rates of compensation).

____ Copies of any pension and/or profit sharing plans.

____ Copies of all insurance policies.

____ Accounts receivable aging report.

____ Inventory information.

____ Assets not appearing on the balance sheet.

____ Brochures, ads, articles, etc.

____ List of any contracts for services.

Chapter 7:
Who Are You Going to Sell To?

When sellers engage with Aberdeen Advisors, they often-times think they "know" who the buyer is going to be. By that, I don't mean they know the actual name of the person or company that will ultimately purchase their company, but that they feel like they know the type of buyer. It's always a little funny when the successful buyer is a type of buyer the seller never knew existed or certainly hadn't considered a legitimate buyer for his type of business.

As you might imagine, different types of buyers look for different things. What is important to one buyer segment may be less important to another. At the end of the day, who/what type of buyer you sell your business to will further determine the steps needed to prepare your business for the sale. There are six primary buyer segments:

- Family Members
- Key Employees

- Competitors/Strategic Buyers
- Private Equity/Financial Buyers
- Family Offices
- Individual Investors

Family Members

Usually, the first buyer preference for business owners is selling to their children or to other family members. While this may seem like a fairly innocuous proposition, especially if the family member is the seller's child, this choice can be magnificent or disastrous —it's usually one of the two. Sometimes I'll be sitting with a family and Mom will tell Dad, "Johnny can't run the business—he has a drug or alcohol problem," or "Johnny is lazy." Dad has run the business, and worked hard through a lot of tough times; Johnny benefited from his father's hard work but doesn't want any part of it for himself.

Often, the children will have a mentality of, "I'll take it if you're giving it to me, but I'm not going to pay you for it." That's not always the case. It's always really refreshing to see the son or daughter say, "I want the business. I'm going to take care of it." A lot of times the next generation may run the business better than the founder; they may have the desire to expand the business' product or service offerings, or to expand the geographies, and so on. This is very rewarding to witness. Unfortunately, such a scenario tends to be an exception to the rule.

In most cases, if you are selling to a family member, you won't need an M&A firm or advisor because the transaction is internal. You can often work with your attorney to manage the deal. Consequently, in the event that there are challenging family dynamics, Aberdeen has successfully been involved to help mitigate emotions and to help the parties focus on the business elements of the transaction. To reiterate, while selling to a family member can be hugely gratifying, please remember that it can also be a very emotional and daunting process.

One such case was a husband-and-wife-owned manufacturing company. The couple came to me and said, "We're going to sell it to our sons." They told me the sons were going to buy it for one million dollars, financed over a 10-year period. It was worth five million dollars, but they were giving them a deal. They asked me, "Can you talk to the boys about this?"

I met with their sons and they said, "We are never going to pay that much for this business." I showed them the valuation, I reiterated that the business was worth five million dollars. It was a no-brainer, the kids should have taken it, but they didn't want it. I went back to the parents and said, "They're not going to buy it." It was like the two sides had never talked. Their family dynamic required a third party with whom to express their honest thoughts.

Dad was determined, "I want my boys to own this business." Mom said, "It's okay. Let's move on." Ultimately, the boys moved on, and the parents got a nice retirement. It took four years to sell the business, but they got almost five million dollars for it.

Key Employees

Key employees can be a great buyer option for business owners. However, selling to a key employee can be particularly challenging based on a number of factors, the foremost being the financing obstacle. An employee may express his delight in the opportunity to purchase the business, however, once the discussion turns to purchase price, oftentimes the employee will need to secure third party financing or the seller will need to extend seller financing.

As the seller, you may not be willing to seller finance over five or ten years. After all, you were most likely planning on receiving a liquidity event of some kind in the first place. In addition to the seller financing challenge, another challenge is that when selling your business, it is necessary to disclose all aspects of the operation including, but not limited to, your salary and the benefits you receive from the company. When selling to a key employee who perhaps may not have had previous access to such confidential information, you run the risk of having that employee share your personal owner benefits with other key employees. Another risk is creating a disgruntled employee because said employee feels he is deserving of a higher compensation, if you're being compensated with "x." You may be thinking that the employee cannot share such sensitive information without consequence; while it is true that anyone who receives confidential information is under a non-disclosure agreement, it goes to that old adage, "once the cat is out of the bag, you can't put it back in the bag."

On the other hand, it is possible to complete a successful transaction with a key employee. I recently helped a client sell his business to a key employee who didn't initially have any money. He got his father-in-law to put money in, then he borrowed the rest from the bank, and he made the deal happen. The seller is happy, and the buyer is thrilled. If the key employee is the right buyer and both parties are realistic, but flexible, odds are the transaction can get done.

Competitors & Strategic Buyers

Negotiating with competitors can be really challenging, because they always think they know more than you. Generally, you're going to a bigger competitor that can afford to buy your business; they probably have (or think they have) a more elite staff, more sophisticated systems, and more industry knowledge. Due to their position, they often undervalue what the business is worth. If they don't go forward with buying your business— which is going to happen more often than not—you've given your competitor all of your information. They know your staff, and they know your customers. Further, they know your strengths and your weaknesses even better than they may have before.

Nevertheless, there can be significant incentive for competitors to follow through with acquiring your business, which could drive up the sale price. A strategic buyer based all over the country, for example, but without a presence in your community, doesn't have the key customers that your company is likely to have. For them to get into your market, they would have to acquire customers account by account, which could take years. If they buy your business, they automatically have established, key customers.

Selling to a competitor can be the biggest opportunity you have to get the most for your business; your competitors understand your industry. They have native knowledge of the industry and perhaps have relationships with a multitude of buyers of your product/service that you haven't tapped into yet and vice versa.

I sold the largest commercial lawn care company in Tampa to the largest lawn care company in the world, out of Los Angeles. They were a billion-dollar, international company, with majority private equity ownership and minority family founder ownership. My client's company, at its peak, hit $20 million in sales. The owner didn't want to sell when I first met him; he had hired me to help buy some companies. I explained to the owner that there were a lot of acquisitive buyers currently in his industry, and asked if he would be interested in selling. Initially, having built the company for more than 20 years (actually starting what would become the company when he was only 12 years old) he emphatically told me, "No, absolutely not." Then, curious that there really were interested buyers, he asked, "What do you think they'd pay me for it?" After performing a financial recap on the company, we came back and told him five or six million dollars. He replied, "That's not enough. I'd never sell for that."

After contemplating the money, and also after having just begun to see the light at the end of the tunnel after the country's worst recession in history, he ultimately hired Aberdeen to sell his company. Our firm presented the company to only a handful of strategic buyers. Literally, within a few days, the founder and CEO of the largest commercial landscape firm in the world approached us and said, "If you show this to another one of my competitors, my price will go down." We said, "Okay, we'll give you a week to get us an acceptable letter of intent that we'll sign." Four days later, we were under contract with the industry's largest, most recognized player. That was incredibly fast. I can't tell that story too many times, because people will think, "Oh, boy, he'll do that for me." It's not realistic, but it is possible and it did happen!

In this case, this strategic buyer with a global presence actually purchased two landscape contracting firms on the exact same day, making Tampa their largest market, overnight. The buyer already had a presence, though declining in the Tampa market, but the acquisitions allowed the buyer to keep its primary competitor OUT of Tampa Bay. Additionally, each company purchased had multiple locations, some in different geographies of the state which allowed the buyer to increase its market share locally, regionally, and nationally. All of these factors fueled the motivation for the buyer. Hence, the buyer was willing to pay substantially more for the business(es). For the company that Aberdeen represented, the seller received double the industry multiple he would have received in the event that the buyer had not been a strategic.

Whatever the motivation, strategic buyers MOST always pay more to get what they want.

Private Equity Firms

A private equity firm is, by definition, a firm set up to invest equity into private businesses. Because of the amount of capital the private equity groups generally have, they want to invest larger amounts of money into stable and growing companies.

Private equity firms have a lot of money; they are built to buy. Some people call them vulture capitalists; they're venture capitalists, but they are sharks. They have strong teams, with their own lawyers and accountants. They are strategic, and they are smart; they are going to ask you one million questions before they give you an offer, and then ten million more questions after you get the offer. Their due diligence process is going to be extremely thorough, but they are probably going to offer you what your business is worth, or more in some cases. They will only buy if it makes fiscal sense; they're in business to make a return on their investors' money.

A trend that has emerged in recent years are private equity funds. These consist of people with an historical amount of capital that say, "We're going to put $100 million into buying businesses." These are often run by retired Baby Boomers, who don't want to sit around and do nothing.

These buyers often ask me, "What's a hot industry?" I tell them I cannot name one industry that's not consolidating—banking, airlines, dry cleaning, commercial lawn care, plumbing. Big money is buying all of these up, because they can get better scale and better profitability. They don't need five CFOs, so they put the companies together. They only need one website. They need one CPA. This trend is contributing to the seller's market we have today, and may make it beneficial for you to sell your business to a private equity investor.

Family Offices

Family offices are private wealth management groups that serve extremely high-net-worth investors. According to a 2016 study by Axial, there is a growing trend in which family offices are directly buying or investing in private companies, as opposed to allocating capital to managers of private equity funds.

Family offices are able to distinguish themselves from traditional private equity firms by sourcing their own investment deals and possessing the ability to close transactions more expeditiously without leveraging. Simply stated and among other key roles, family offices manage the financial and investment side of an affluent individual or family. They may also offer such services as budgeting, insurance management, and so on but ultimately, they combine asset management, cash management, and financial management to help very wealthy families in their overall wealth management.

A family office may serve as a great prospective buyer for your company. There is a trend towards family offices being very acquisitive and directly buying companies. A family office buyer will value your company for the long run, will likely be more willing to work with existing management (versus bringing in their own executives or drastically cutting staff), and has the ability to close the transaction quickly with their own cash, so no third party lending source is required.

Over the years, our firm has noted a significant increase in the number of family offices attempting to source deals directly through us. From our experience, working with family offices has many advantages but perhaps most importantly, we typically communicate with the top decision maker from the onset. Family offices are therefore able to make a decision very quickly on whether to move forward or not on a particular transaction. This saves everyone time and ultimately, money.

Individual Entrepreneur or Investor

Our firm often deals with the individual entrepreneur seeking a business to purchase and operate. This can be an ideal scenario for a smaller business, wherein the seller is willing to stay onboard for an extended period of time to help with the transition. Although these situations can be ideal for the seller, they are not without challenges.

For example, very similar to a key employee as a buyer situation, individual buyers may not have the cash to purchase your business for what it is truly worth. Therefore, they seek third party financing such as an SBA (Small Business Association) loan or a conventional loan, both of which will require seller financing. Additionally, when dealing with a lender such as a bank, the sales process can be exhausting and you may not know if the buyer is approved for the purchase price until weeks, or even months, after you've entered into a contract. Traditionally, letters of intent include an exclusivity clause which will require you to take your business off the market while the buyer is conducting due diligence and going through the bank approval process.

Fortunately, for Aberdeen clients, we have had much success in getting through the third party lending process. From the business valuation required by banks, through due diligence and ultimately, through the finer details such as negotiating working capital, finalizing inventory, agreeing on employment contracts, securing the transfer of third party leases, and so on, Aberdeen has successfully assisted in working through all aspects of the process with the individual buyer and his lending institution.

In addition to the financing component, there is also the training aspect as with any buyer. However, with the individual buyer, training can be especially cumbersome. The successful buyer may or may not possess your industry experience, or may be a first-time business owner. Individual buyers often successfully purchase and thrive, however, as part of the seller vetting process, you will want to make sure that in addition to the financing component, you are comfortable with the buyer and his ultimate purchase of your company.

Should You Sell Part of Your Business to an Investor?

A lot of equity firms will want you to keep a percentage of your company. They want to be aligned with management, so instead of getting a full 100% buyout, you may be only selling 60 or 70% of your business. That can be great, because if you grow that business with the equity firm, you may get a lot more for your business. Of course, you could also get less if it doesn't work out.

Here's how it works. You may have heard the phrase, "There is so much cash on the sidelines." Many people do not believe there is much cash waiting to be deployed, but in fact, there is. The amount of cash that companies and investment funds have is staggering.

Let's look at some of the facts. According to a 2014 article published in the Wall Street Journal, there are over 30 private equity firms in the United States with over one trillion dollars of buying power. Corporations have over three trillion dollars in cash on their corporate balance sheets. As a result, these funds and corporations are becoming more aggressive in finding businesses to purchase since they need a return on their investment.

So, with that much cash on the sidelines, how can you take advantage of this opportunity? Of course, you do not have to do anything; you may choose to stay the course and sell 100% of your business so you can fully retire. However, if you're not quite ready to retire and are looking to grow your business, you can use an investor or private equity firm to help fund your growth plan and share in the upside with you.

Let's say that your business is worth $10 million. The private equity group makes an offer to buy 60% of your company for $6 million, and you keep 40% of the company. You can continue to run the business, and now you have a capital partner backing you. Not to mention, you get $6 million less any transaction fees and payoff of debts.

Different private equity groups have different strategies. They may come in and hire a Chief Financial Officer, bring in a CEO, they'll get the books audited, they'll put the IT in the Cloud. Now the business is worth eight times cash flow because they've fixed the business, they've made it more valuable. The idea is to grow your company, and one day you and your new partner can sell the company for a much larger number. So if you sell the business later for $50 million and you own 40% of the company, then you make another $20 million plus the $6 million you made on the first partial sale of the business.

The key is finding the right capital partner that will not only provide capital, but also help you strategically grow the company, making it larger and more profitable. Private equity groups can help you expand locations, buy additional companies within your industry, and hire senior staff members.

That being said, there are potential downfalls. One is the possible loss of control. Many funds will look at minority investments, but most of them want majority control. So you may still be President and running the day-to-day activities, but legally, they have control. This issue seems to be one of the biggest reasons I see owners decide not to move forward. So before you embark on the process of finding the right partner, please make sure you are ready to have a new partner.

Another big risk is that you may not get along with your new capital partner, and you could either be unhappy or get fired. These are simply some of the risks you must be willing to take when utilizing a strategy like this one. If you have the right partner and the right plan, and you execute it well, everything could work out fine. If you don't have the right partner, the right plan or proper implementation, then this strategy will be challenging.

Punching Around in the Dark

So how do you navigate all of these choices? How do you know which option is the best for you and your business? Business owners often come to us "punching around in the dark." They've been trying to sell or trying to figure the answer to this question out for a while.

They started looking for a buyer; they got a letter in the mail or they get a phone call. It may be a buyer, but it may not be an ideal buyer. They're certainly not hearing from multiple ideal buyers. They meet with the buyer, but he's not going to pay them what they want or they don't like the guy. "This is harder than I thought it was going to be," they think. They finally come to the realization say, after six years, that they do need help.

For most of them, selling a business is a once in a lifetime event. It's one of the most important financial decisions they'll make in their life, because their future is so tied to their business. This is their retirement money. This is the money they want to use to live out their motivation—to travel with their wife, to see the grandkids in Canada and Boston.

Why would you undertake such a significant decision by yourself? Hiring a qualified M&A advisor is what's going to set you, your family, and your legacy up for success.

PART II:
SIX STEPS TO SOLD

CHAPTER 8:

Working with an M&A Advisor

According to a recent study by the Business Enterprise Institute (2015), 69% of all business owners in the United States plan to exit their business within the next ten years. However, only 15% of those business owners have sought advice from advisors and begun the exit planning process. These statistics typify how few business owners actually plan out their departure from their businesses. The truth of the matter is, every business owner will eventually exit his business. It is up to you to decide what options and opportunities you may have in doing so.

I advise clients to take control of their future and invest the time to create the most options for themselves and for their families. Furthermore, given that your exit from your company is likely to be the most significant financial event of your life, why wouldn't you hire an expert to guide you through cashing out your business? This chapter helps you to differentiate among the various types of advisors. Based on your own personal situation, it can help you determine which type of advisor would be the most advantageous to you. Whether it be an expert M&A advisor or an investment banker, it is advisable for you to seek the assistance of a third party to guide you through the process of turning your blood, sweat and tears into cash.

M&A Firms and Investment Bankers

According to a study by Fairfield University professor Dr. Michael McDonald, titled "The Value of Middle-Market Investment Bankers," 100% of owners who sold their business with the help of an investment banker said that hiring an advisor added value—69% of the 85 business owners surveyed went so far as to say the advisor added "significant value" to the transaction.

At Aberdeen Advisors, we are not investment bankers—investment bankers provide advisory services to companies over $50 million. They require a substantial retainer, an ongoing monthly fee, and the overall costs are usually significantly higher due to overhead, legal and auditing requirements, and the size of the deal team. However, M&A advisory firms such as ours perform much the same work, at a significantly lower fee.

The study revealed that working with an M&A advisor helped sellers to overcome obstacles inherent to middle-market businesses such as:

- **Determining the true value of their business**
- **Uncovering middle market M&A transaction data**
- **Balancing the demands of the sale with day-to-day operations**
- **Finding the right buyer at the best price**

"Managing the M&A process" was found to be the most valuable service the investment banker and M&A advisors provide. This includes organizing a go-to-market plan and executing on that plan, including creating teasers and confidential memorandums, managing single or multiple data rooms, negotiating key terms and conditions, and managing the sales process to a timeline.

Business owners also rely heavily on advisors to negotiate the transaction, prepare the company for sale, and add credibility to their profile as a seller.

"Aberdeen definitely got us more offers, a higher sales price, and the most favorable terms based on what we wanted to do post closing," noted an Aberdeen client (the owner of a manufacturing company).

Another Aberdeen client commented, "After trying to sell my company myself, I finally realized it was near impossible to run my business and try to sell it myself at the same time. The Aberdeen team eased my burden and allowed me to focus on sustaining and growing my business while they devoted time to selling the company. By staying focused on the business, I was able to make sure my sales and profitability didn't slide while going through the process."

Another key finding that the study revealed, which was conducted between 2011 and 2016, was that for 84% of the business owners, their final sale price was equal to or higher than the initial sale price estimate provided by the investment banker or M&A advisor.

Transaction Fees

Transaction fees vary widely from firm to firm but are typically based on the size of the transaction and the services provided. The typical investment banker fee is usually much higher than that of a firm such as Aberdeen. For instance, an investment banking firm generally charges an upfront retainer fee PLUS a monthly fee. These fees vary but can run from a few thousand dollars to hundreds of thousands of dollars based on the size of your company.

At Aberdeen, as we've mentioned, we operate primarily on a success-fee business model. Generally, we only get paid if we sell your business; there are no upfront fees or hidden costs to our sellers. As you may imagine, this can be a risky proposition. We could spend an inordinate amount of time on a company and then have something that is out of our (or the seller's) control disrupt the industry and significantly reduce the value of the company or worse, render it un-sellable. This has happened to our firm. Consequently, we are confident in our ability to achieve successful outcomes. Hence, it has historically been our business model to enter into success-fee-only engagements.

With a success-fee-only business model, it is imperative that our firm thoroughly vets prospective sellers. Back to the motivation question posed previously; if a seller is not 100% motivated, it is not worth our time to secure the engagement.

Specifically, our fees are based on the size of the company to be sold and whether or not real estate will be included in the transaction. Typical fees range from five to ten percent on most transactions. The fees are based on the total transaction value to include but not be limited to, the purchase price in its entirety.

What to Expect if Working with Aberdeen

At Aberdeen, we are not business brokers. We are not investment bankers. And we're not your typical Mergers and Acquisitions firm.

We've been in your shoes. We've experienced first-hand the emotional, physical, and financial roller coaster of building, operating, and selling a business. This unique perspective is backed by decades of experience in the business world, from marketing and management to business development and consulting. Our advisors have worked with some of the largest companies in the world. We are highly skilled at managing every aspect of complex deals often associated with the sale of mid-market firms. We are experts at pinpointing your challenges and navigating them skillfully to create opportunities.

You likely have various options when it comes to hiring an advisor. If you decide to work with Aberdeen, you can take comfort in knowing that 96% of our clients have stated that they would refer us to another business owner. In addition, 98% of them would use Aberdeen again. We are proud of our track record, and the strategies and skills we have honed over the years to yield the best results for our clients.

Over the course of closing hundreds of successful business transactions, we've architected a unique six-step process designed to help business owners find the right buyer, and ultimately get the highest sales price for their business. And as former business owners ourselves, it's a process we've designed with your unique needs in mind.

We know better than anyone that you're not just selling your business. You're looking to free yourself. You're ready to make your exit strategy a reality. You're passing on a legacy you've worked hard to build. You're making a smart financial decision to help ensure your future and your family's future. It's why your dedicated mergers and acquisitions team will be there to guide you every step of the way, helping you position your business properly, pinpoint and motivate ideal buyers and close the best possible deal on your behalf.

Our process can be broken down into six phases:

ABERDEEN'S "SIX STEPS TO SOLD"

The six-step proprietary process
that's helped us close hundreds of
transactions

Average Time from Engagement to Close: 9-12 months.

Serious Results for Serious Sellers.

Phase I = Strategize

Phase II = Position

Phase III = Market

Phase IV = Negotiate

Phase V = Deliver

Phase VI = Close

You can expect the first four phases to take zero to six months, and due diligence another two to to four months. Then you're closing. It is important to note that transaction size, sophistication of the buyer, and the source of capital all have the potential to significantly impact the length of time to close a transaction.

For example, for larger companies, a sophisticated buyer may require audited financial statements or a quality of earnings report. If the seller doesn't already have audited financials statements, this time-intensive process can substantially lengthen the due diligence process. Additionally, for buyers who opt to go the SBA financing route, this process can also be a time drain. However, it is important to note that the more prepared you are as a seller in terms of having your financial house in order, the less time the due diligence process may take.

Strategize

The first step to putting your best foot forward in the marketplace is to conduct a business valuation. You will also evaluate a variety of key issues such as financial performance, seller expectations, customer concentration, supplier concentration, management team, transition and you will devise a final exit strategy.

Position

Next, your Aberdeen advisory team will develop confidential marketing materials designed to intrigue and motivate ideal buyers, without revealing business specifics. As former business owners, we understand the sensitive nature of this process for both you, your employees, your customers and suppliers.

Market

Our philosophy is simple. The right competition for your business yields superior results. One buyer is good. One buyer that is ideal for your business is even better. But multiple ideal buyers? That's the goal your dedicated advisor will stop at nothing to achieve — and it's part of the reason Aberdeen's 83% close rate is far above the industry average of 25%. Through a careful screening process, we strategically pinpoint ideal buyers, discreetly distributing your marketing materials and monitoring buyer interest through confidential discussions.

Negotiate

Your team will guide you through the process of handling multiple offers and moving multiple ideal buyers toward stronger offers.

Deliver

Due diligence is perhaps the most underestimated step of the entire process. Many business owners may not realize that during this critical process, approximately half of all deals fall apart. It's where Aberdeen Advisors once again separates itself from the industry, navigating this delicate process with the necessary skill and organization to deliver a signed, sealed contract.

Close

Take a deep breath — you're now officially free to pursue whatever goal brought you to us in the first place.

Let's take a deeper look at each of these phases in the following six chapters.

CHAPTER 9:
Step 1 – Strategize

ABERDEEN'S "SIX STEPS TO SOLD"

The six-step proprietary process that's helped us close hundreds of transactions

Strategize > Position > Market > Negotiate > Deliver > Close

Business Valuation
Address Key Issues
- Financial perfomance
- Seller expectations
- Positioning
- Customer concentration
- Manage team
- Transition
- Final exit strategy

Serious Results for Serious Sellers.

This step typically takes less than a month. However, it can be drawn out, based upon how prepared the client is. Once the seller submits the required information to our team, this phase takes a couple of weeks.

As much as you may want to undertake this step on your own, you really need to have a trusted advisor, a lawyer, and a CPA to strategize the sale of your business. As M&A advisors, we really hold a mirror up to your business to reflect what potential buyers will see and what they want to see—that you may not be prepared to show them.

At Aberdeen, we hold a strategy session with potential clients before we agree to take them on. The purpose of this session is to make sure that we think we can sell their business, and that we are aligned in our goals and expectations. We want to feel confident we are working with good people and good businesses who have nothing to hide, because if something goes bad we could get sued, just as they could.

We hold ourselves to a high ethical standard. We make sure that standards such as the following are met:

- **Your corporation is active. We can't sell your company if you haven't paid your annual Secretary of State bill this year. We ask for all these documents.**

- **We look at your tax returns and see how they compare to your financial statements. If you come in and say, "Oh, I know it says I didn't make any money, but I take about three hundred thousand in cash that I don't report." We won't take you on as a client.**

- **Your books are a mess. You need to get a CPA to clean them up.**

In this session, we are looking to analyze the business's strengths and weaknesses before we move forward. At the first meeting we ask the seller to tell us about the company, tell us about the people, tell us about the customers, and tell us about the competition. We are looking at the business from a buyer's perspective, a bank's perspective, and a business planning perspective.

The first task we focus on is the business valuation.

Business Valuation

Our firm is not certified to do full business valuations, but based on the company's cash flow and other circumstances, we can offer our opinion of value.

We do a pretty deep dive. We will look at the company's tax returns, financials, and margins. The businesses we sell are multiples of cash flow. If the client is a doctor and he has $1 million in revenue but he takes home $500,000—$500,000 is his cash flow.

Our bigger businesses are sold on a multiple of EBITDA. EBITDA is an acronym for "earnings before interest, taxes, depreciation, and amortization." The number is, effectively, the cash flow of the business—what you are going to have in profit, or cash, to take home every year to pay down debt.

EBITDA shows you a debt-free company's profit. We typically sell companies for four to six times EBITDA; the bigger companies will sell for higher. The multiple is based on the risk to the buyer. The lower the risk, the higher the multiple, the higher the valuation. Let me give you an example.

Let's say we have a manufacturing company that makes $20 million per year in revenue. They have a 15% profit margin, or profit to the bottom line, which means they would have $3 million in cash flow. The business would sell for five or six times EBITDA, or $15 to 18 million.

Then we'd come in and go, "It looks like you haven't painted the building in 30 years. Your software is outdated. You don't really have a management team." Or the exact opposite, "Wow, brand new roof, state of the art software, audited financials. You're going to be on the higher end of the industry average, maybe even outside the number I just gave you."

If a client says they'd like to get more than the valuation we give them, we tell them, "Okay, that is possible if your business continues to grow, you expand your customer base, and you expand your margins." If the client can only sell the business for their target number, I'd say, "Let's wait and continue to grow it." If we don't think we could meet their expectation, we tell them that up front. If he is willing to accept the valuation rate—though hopefully, we'll get higher—then we'll proceed. We put an agreement in place, and a success-fee base to move forward.

Many clients will ask, "What can I do to drive valuation?" As the risk to the buyer goes up, the value to your business goes down. If you lower the risk, the multiple goes up and the value goes up. One way to demonstrate level of risk is to get your financials reviewed or audited. At the end of the day, the buyer is going to have this done anyway, so you might as well go ahead and get it cleaned up for them. Less than 5% of sellers end up taking this advice, even though we tell them, "You're going to get more money. It's going to make it easier." Trust us, it's good advice.

If you hire a valuation company to get a third party valuation, it will typically cost from $5,000 to $10,000. They will look at the business's management team, the industry, the growth rate, and the financials. If you have a patent, that will drive your number. Your equipment will drive your number, and your employees and your strategy will drive your number.

The company would then come back and say, "Your business is worth $7,000,232." That's a great first step to have even before you come to us, because now you have a certified appraisal for what your business is worth. It doesn't mean you're going to sell it for that amount, but at least you have a value, based on your industry.

Sometimes we'll also do a real estate appraisal, or an assessment on the environmental. It's the sellers who take these extra steps that are going to have a great outcome.

Top Ten Critical Factors that Impact the Value of a Business

If you focus on improving each of these areas, you can expect a higher value for your business.

1. Cash Flow

Cash is king! The more profits your company generates, the more valuable your business. Most businesses are run to minimize the tax hit from Uncle Sam, and to maximize the cash flow to the business owner. So, financial statements are "recast" to reflect what the true profits of the business are. For example, if you recast the profits of the business by taking out the car and airplane expense for the business owner, it may dramatically change the cash flow picture. Most businesses are valued based on a multiple of cash flow (or Earnings Before Interest Taxes Depreciation and Amortization "EBITDA"). The higher the cash flow, the higher the multiplier on the cash flow.

2. Growth Trends

If your business is steadily growing, then the business will have a higher value. If the trends are negative, then there will be a fairly big impact to the value in most cases.

3. Recurring Revenue

If your company has recurring revenue, then you should receive a higher value for your business. Why? Because the new buyer knows that every month they too will receive that income. For example, pest control businesses have a recurring revenue model. The pest control company will spray your house or business every month. This is predictable revenue and profits.

4. Customer Concentration

If Walmart is your largest customer and accounts for 50% of your sales, then your business has too much customer concentration. Buyers would like to see a more diversified customer base so that the impact of the loss of one customer is not devastating to the business.

5. Impact of the Business Owner Leaving the Business

This is a common problem with businesses under $10 million in revenue. The business is centered on the business owner. That is wonderful until you want to sell the business. All the customers and suppliers want to work with the owner. This can be a problem for a new buyer.

6. Management Team

A good management team can not only improve the company, but it also improves the value of the business.

7. Margins

The higher the gross profit margins and net income margins, the higher the business valuation. There is more cash flow with higher margins. Additionally, the lower margins highlight a tough, competitive climate.

8. Industry

If you are in the social media industry like Facebook or Google, congratulations, you are about to be very rich! This industry is considered a "hot" industry. The industry you are in does matter. As of early 2017, hotels are hot. Drones are hot. There are many industries that cycle up and down with the market.

9. Accounting Records

Having a good CPA firm and good internal accounting records affect the value of your business. Ask any business owner who just sold his business and you'll find he spent a lot of time in due diligence in this one area.

10. Fair Market Value of the Company's Assets

Some companies and industries have a lot of hard assets. This should improve their valuation as long as these assets generate cash flow for the company.

Discussion of Key Issues

As part of Aberdeen's business valuation process, there are several key issues we discuss with our clients that will drive the valuation.

- The stronger the management team, the higher the valuation.
- The better the financials, the higher the valuation.
- The less customer concentration, the higher the value.
- The greater the profit margins, the higher the value.

- The higher the growth rate, the higher the margin.
- The better the industry is growing, the higher the valuation.

All of these factors are going to be plus or minus, based on where they are versus their peers.

Management Team

Whether the business will maintain members of the management team is critical, especially if the owner is going to be gone. I have one client now where three out of the four family members are going to leave after closing. The buyer says, "That may not be a big deal to you, but to us, that's a huge deal. You're taking 75% of the management out the day after—or six months— after closing." He knows that they're a well-vested management team because they're family members; the risk goes up by losing those key players.

Another of my clients is a big surgeon; he's the rain maker, but his business has five other doctors. He does 78% of the revenue, which is not great, but at least I can show a buyer, "Look, 22% is coming from other doctors and we are hiring other surgeons, so he's becoming less and less of this overall pie." As part of our strategy session, we would discuss how they could start to increase the advertising for the other five doctors; he could also hire more doctors.

In another situation, a seller might say "Everybody's been here 20 or 30 years, and they play to stay." I'll say, "Great, give me their names, roles and responsibilities, how long they've each been with the company, and the strengths of each person."

If their team has a long tenure like that, we're going to want to play that up; it shows a very stable company. It reduces the risk and increases the value for a buyer if they have a really strong operations person, a really strong financial person, a really strong sales manager, and a good marketing person.

Financials

Let's say we look at the financials and the tax returns are done on cash, and the financials are done on accrual basis. That's okay, but we're going to have to explain that to a buyer. We're going to dig in and make sure we understand those adjustments from cash to accrual, so that we can explain it properly.

We're going to look at how much bad debt they have, and if they have any legal lawsuits pending or threatened. We're going to look at non-competes.

Because buyers will be very interested in your historical financials as well as your current statements, you will want to begin the process of legitimizing your financials well in advance of a sale. Even if you feel like your internal accounting staff or bookkeeper does a meticulous job, by having the financials reviewed or audited by a reputable CPA firm, you will not only drive the value of the company but will also save yourself many headaches by addressing any unforeseen issues once the company has already gone to market.

Seller's Expectations

The seller's expectations will be more intimately discussed in Chapter 12, but here is where we get a broad overview of what the seller desires in terms of the type of buyer, his plans post transaction, and the seller's flexibility regarding the structure of an offer. We will ask questions such as: Will you accept all cash? Will you accept a seller note? Will you take stock? The seller's answers will help determine if he is a client Aberdeen will take on.

Customer Concentration

The lower the concentration one customer has, the better. The more diverse they are, the higher the value. If you have one customer, you're going to get a low valuation and they're not going to pay you all cash, because if you lose that customer, you've lost the business.

I'll ask, "Tell me your top customer. What percentage of revenue is that?" They may say that client is 40%. "What's your second client?" Perhaps it's 10%." "What about your third?" Maybe another 10%. Now I know that there's 60% of the revenue within three clients, which is a major weakness. It's going to impact valuation, and it's probably going to impact how much cash they get at closing. If they give me these percentages, I'm likely going to ask them for the last two or three years' revenue per client so that we can really dig deeper.

I will ask, "What are you doing from a sales and marketing standpoint to diversify your customer base?" If they're not doing anything or they don't have a plan, we will help come up with a plan to diversify. Our goal is to take each weakness and make a plan to correct it.

Transition and Exit Strategy

In addition to verifying if the management team is going to stay on after the sale, we need to know if the seller intends to stay on through a transition period. If you're going to leave the day after close, you're going to get less value than if you stay and help the buyer over time.

The exit strategy determines if your plans are to go public, to sell to a competitor, or to perhaps sell to an employee.

Those are key issues under the business valuation, and we will strategize with the seller prior to going through the process so that they're prepared and we can use that information to help position the company.

In our many years of doing this work, we have determined that to have the best outcome, this is the best process. We have refined the process over the years, but this system is what's going to produce the best results; it has helped us close hundreds of transactions and created why we've been so successful.

CHAPTER 10:
Phase II -Position

The six-step proprietary process that's helped us close hundreds of transactions

Strategize · Position · Market · Negotiate · Deliver · Close

Create CONFIDENTIAL Marketing Materials
- One-page Teaser
- Confidential Memorandum

At this phase, we've determined that we want to work with the client and we are under contract to sell their business. We now review the financials for at least the previous three years, and we begin the development of marketing collateral materials that are designed to intrigue and motivate ideal buyers, without revealing business specifics. This phase typically takes a few weeks.

In the initial strategy session, we looked at the strengths and weaknesses of the company. Now we want to properly position it to the marketplace. We'll do that in several different ways.

For example, you may be a manufacturer and a distribution company. We know that we could get a higher multiple for the business if we position it as a high-tech manufacturing company versus a high-tech distribution company. Positioning an ad agency as a digital agency will also earn a higher multiple. This is where it pays to have experts on your team.

We could also strategize positioning certain factors in your business, such as a really strong management team. We take the big attributes and say, "This is why you should pay a lot for this business: very diversified customer base, great management team." The goal is to emphasize the business's strengths. We can show the weaknesses as well, but we need to address what is being done to counteract those weaknesses.

Create a Teaser

The first step is to create a teaser. This is a blind summary that will explain the industry and what the opportunity is,

ACQUISITION OPPORTUNITY

Introduction

Aberdeen Advisors has been exclusively engaged to sell a southeastern market leader in the business services industry. The Company offers outstanding financial performance, and a multitude of growth and expansion opportunities.

After posting revenues of around $15M for 2014 and 2015, the Company forecasts 2016 revenues in the $20M range with an adjusted EBITDA of approximately 10%.

The owners are seeking 100% buyout and the transaction includes all inventory and equipment. The real estate currently occupied by the Company is not included in this offering, but available for purchase as a separate transaction.

Investment Highlights

Established Market Position

By leveraging its strong partnerships with quality suppliers and its large referral base of satisfied customers, the Company will continue to be a major player within the market. With motivated new ownership commited to enhancing its sales and marketing efforts, its extensive product line and substantial expertise will help it to outpace its competition.

Geographic Expansion Opportunities

By implementing a growth startegy aimed at geographic expansion, new ownership could realize quick revenue growth. Growth could be achieved through greater expansion into the commercial market, as well as pursuit of synergistic partnerships with related players within the industry. Additionally, acquisition growth could serve to reduce regional competition and thereby expand the Company's geographic footprint.

Financial Performance

Revenue & Adjusted EBITDA Trend

The Company's earnings have grown significantly over the last several years and are projected to be in the $20M range in 2016.

Aberdeen Advisors has been engaged to sell 100% of this business. Please contact Emery Ellinger at 727-639-4716 or *emery@aberdeenadvisors.com* with any questions.

that we can send to qualified buyers and funds to determine if they have an interest. With this method, they never know which company is being sold. As former business owners, the Aberdeen team understands the sensitive nature of this process for you, your employees, your customers and suppliers. If the blind summary attracts a potential buyer, they can look at it and say, "Yes, I'd like to find out more." Then they would sign a non-disclosure—or confidentiality—form, and we would send them a confidential information memorandum.

The teaser on the previous page is an example created for a window and installation company. Following is a sample confidentiality agreement.

STANDARD BUYER'S CONFIDENTIALITY AND WARRANTY AGREEMENT

The undersigned (the "Buyer") understands and acknowledges that Aberdeen Advisors, Inc. (the "Broker" has a valid agreement with the owner(s) (the "Seller") of the business and/or property described below (the "Business") whereby Broker has been retained, for an agreed upon commission, to represent Seller in the sale of the Business. Buyer understands and acknowledges the Broker is acting as the agent of the Seller and that Broker's primary duty is to represent the interests of the Seller. The Business that is the subject of this Standard Buyer's Confidentiality and Warrant Agreement (the "Agreement") is as follows:

Description of Business: Promotional Products company and real estate in St. Petersburg, Florida

In order to induce Broker or Seller to furnish information regarding the Business (the "Information") to Buyer for Buyer's evaluation and possible purchase of said Business and in consideration for Broker's or Seller's furnishing such information, Buyer understands, agrees, represents and warrants to Broker and Seller as follows:

1. The word "Buyer," as used herein, shall mean and include the undersigned individually, as a member of a partnership, as an employee, stockholder, officer or director of a corporation, as an agent, advisor or consultant for or to any business entity and in any other capacity whatsoever.

2. The Information is of a proprietary and confidential nature, the disclosure of which to any other party will result in damage to the Seller and/or Business, and Buyer further represents and warrants as follows:

   (A) The Information furnished by Broker or Seller has not been publicly disclosed, has not been made available to Buyer by any party or source other than Broker or Seller and is being furnished only upon the terms and conditions contained in this Agreement.

(B) Buyer will not disclose the Information, in whole or in part, to any party other than persons within Buyer's organization, including independent advisers/consultants, who have a need to know such Information for purposes of evaluating or structuring the possible purchase of the Business. Buyer accepts full responsibility for full compliance with all provisions of this Agreement by such other persons.

(C) Buyer will not disclose, except to the extent required by law, to any parties other than the persons described in Paragraph 2(B) above that the Business is available for purchase or that evaluations, discussions or negotiations are taking place concerning a possible purchase.

(D) Buyer will not utilize, now or at any time in the future, any trade secret(s), as that term may be defined under statutory or common law, that is/are included in the furnished Information for any purpose other than evaluating the possible purchase of the Business, including, without limitation, not utilizing same in the conduct of Buyer's or any other party's present or future business(es).

(E) In addition to the prohibition against utilizing trade secret(s), Buyer will not utilize any other furnished information for any purpose other than evaluating the possible purchase of the Business, specifically including, without limitation, not utilizing same to enter into and/or engage in competition with the Business or assist or promote any other party(s) in so doing. The foregoing prohibition against utilizing said Information in competing with the Business shall remain in effect for three (3) years from the date hereof and shall be applicable to competition within the presently existing marketing area of the Business.

(F) If Buyer decides not to pursue the possible purchase of the Business, Buyer will promptly return to Broker all Information previously furnished by Broker or Seller, including any and all reproductions of same, and further, shall destroy any and all analyses, compilations or other material that incorporates any part of said Information.

3. Buyer will not contact the Seller or Seller's employees, customers, suppliers or agents other than Broker for any reason whatsoever without the prior consent of the Broker. All contacts with the Seller or such other parties will be made through or by Broker unless otherwise agreed to by Broker, in writing.

4. The Information furnished by Broker has been prepared by or is based upon representations of the Seller and Broker has made no independent

investigation or verification of said Information. Buyer hereby expressly releases and discharges Broker from any and all responsibility and/or liability in connection with the accuracy, completeness or any other aspects of the information and accepts sole and final responsibility for the evaluation of the Information and all other factors relating to the Business.

5. The Information is subject to change or withdrawal without notice. Further, the solicitation of offers for the purchase of the Business is subject to withdrawal of such solicitation without notice.

6. Buyer will indemnify and hold harmless the Broker and Seller from any and all claims or actions arising from Buyer's acts or failures to act either of which constitute negligence, gross negligence or intentional misconduct in pursuing the possible purchase of the Business, including, without limitation, reasonable attorney's fees and other expenses incurred by Broker.

7. Buyer will not, for a period of three (3) years from the date hereof, enter into any agreement for the purchase of the Business, in whole or in part, or assist or promote any other party in so doing, unless such agreement to purchase provides for commission to be paid Broker, with the commission being

defined as the amount agreed upon by Broker and Seller in the "Standard Listing Agreement" or similar agreement between those parties. The phrase "agreement for the purchase of the Business" as used herein, shall mean and include any agreement, specifically including, but not limited to, offers to purchase, letters of intent and similar agreements, that provides for the transfer, conveyance, possession of, or disposition of the Business, its capital stock, assets, or any portion thereof, and the commission amount to be paid Broker shall be the greater of either the minimum commission or the commission based upon sale price (or purchase price), as these amounts are defined in the aforesaid agreement between Broker and Seller. Further, "sale price (or purchase price)" as used herein shall mean and include the total amount of consideration paid or conveyed to Seller or for Seller's benefit, including, without limitation, cash, capital stock, notes, personal property of any kind, real property, leases, lines of credit, loans, contingent payments (e.g., license agreements, royalty agreements, payments based upon future sales or profits, etc.), employment or management contracts, consulting agreements, non-competition agreements, assumption or discharge of any or

all liabilities, and any combination of the foregoing and/or other consideration. The commission
amount agreed upon by Broker and Seller in the
aforesaid agreement between those parties will be
made known to Buyer by Broker, upon Buyer's request, when and if an agreement for the purchase
of the Business is made by Buyer. If Buyer violates
the foregoing provision, Buyer will be liable for and
pay said commission to Broker upon demand without any obligation on Broker's part to first exhaust
any legal remedies against Seller.

8. Buyer represents that Buyer has sufficient financial
resources to complete the transaction for the asking price and terms set forth herein. Buyer agrees to
provide, upon request by Broker or Seller, financial
statements, references and other pertinent information evidencing such financial sufficiency.

9. The performance and construction of this Agreement shall be governed by the laws of the State of
Florida. All sums due hereunder shall be payable at
the office of the Broker in Pinellas County, Florida
and all parties hereto agree to forbear from filing a
claim in any other jurisdiction.

10. This Agreement shall be binding upon the Buyer,
Buyer's heirs, executors, successors, assigns, ad-
ministrators or representatives. If any provision

of this Agreement shall be held to be invalid, void or unenforceable, the remainder of the provisions hereof shall remain in full force and effect and this Agreement shall be construed as if such invalid, void or unenforceable provision had not been contained herein.

11. Any controversy between the parties to this Agreement involving the construction or application of any of the terms, covenants or conditions of this Agreement, shall on written request of one (1) party served on the other, be submitted to binding arbitration. Such arbitration shall be under the rules of the American Arbitration Association. The arbitrator shall have no authority to change any provisions of this agreement; the arbitrator's sole authority shall be to interpret or apply the provisions of this Agreement. The expenses of arbitration conducted pursuant to this paragraph shall be born by the parties in such proportion as the Arbitrators shall decide.

12. The terms and conditions of this Agreement shall also apply to any other business and/or property on which Broker has been retained to represent the owner(s) in the sale thereof and on which Broker or owner(s) has furnished information to Buyer. Further, it shall not be necessary for Buyer to

execute any additional agreement(s) to that effect and any terms and conditions of this Agreement that refer to the date hereof shall automatically be adjusted to reflect the date on which Broker or owner(s) initially furnished information to Buyer on such other business and/or property.

13. The provisions hereof cannot be modified, amended, supplemented or rescinded without the written consent of Broker and this Agreement sets forth the entire agreement and understanding

EXECUTED ON THIS _____ DAY OF _____, 2017.

_____	_____
Typed/Printed Name of Buyer	Typed/Printed Name of Buyer
_____	_____
Signature (Individually and as Duly Authorized Representative)	Signature (Individually and as Duly Authorized Representative)
_____	_____
Typed/Printed Name of Signatory	Typed/Printed Name of Signatory
_____	_____
Street Address	Street Address
_____	_____
City, State, Zip Code	City, State, Zip Code
_____	_____
Telephone	Telephone

Form352

The Confidential Information Memorandum

The confidential information memorandum will give a complete overview of the business, and answer questions that a buyer would have before they would actually make an offering. The key is to have buyer-based packaging, meaning it's meant to entice and highlight the strengths of a certain business.

The document includes information on what is being sold. Are you selling the building in real estate? Are you selling a business? Are you selling multiple businesses? What comes with the business? What are the assets? What are the equipment? What's the management team look like? Who's staying? Who's not staying? What's the ownership structure? It may include some pictures of the plant, and give the history of the business.

By the time sellers approach us at Aberdeen, it's likely they've been trying to do this step on their own, in terms of finding qualified buyers—for years, in some cases. However, they probably would not have created a document like this. They would find a buyer and give them the tax returns, and give them some financials, but they wouldn't have a thirty-page memorandum with pictures. A lot of these sellers don't even have great websites. We're going to deliver to the potential buyer a very professional presentation on the seller's business.

Here is an example of a table of contents of a detailed confidential memorandum, created by Aberdeen Advisors for one of our clients.

TABLE OF CONTENTS

Aberdeen *advisors*

CHAPTER 11:
Phase III - Market

Aberdeen's process involves lengthy discussions with our sellers, prior to going to market. We need to understand if there is any buyer or any type of buyer that our seller is

adamantly opposed to selling to. For example, we have some physician sellers who are strongly opposed to selling to a large healthcare entity such as BayCare, while we have other physicians who seek to sell to such a conglomerate. In another industry, we may have a seller who won't sell to a designated competitor based on how that competitor is perceived to treat its employees. Another component to this process is gaining a full understanding of what our seller's goals are for the transaction and post closing.

For instance, if a seller tells me that he is willing to stay onboard for a six month to a year transition period to make sure his successor is properly trained, I know that our buyer pool is much larger than if the seller states he will only provide a 30- to 60-day training period for the new buyer. The seller's desire post transaction is a significant factor in the type of buyer we will target.

In addition to the seller's expectations regarding the type of buyer and plans post transaction, it is important for us to have a clear understanding of the seller's flexibility regarding the structure of an offer. For example, if a seller is emphatic that he will only accept all cash and will not entertain an earn out scenario or any seller financing—even a seller note of less than 10% of the purchase price with a short payback period (i.e. six months)—then the buyer pool is immediately shrunken. Such a scenario is highly possible and our firm has done it successfully many times, it is just important for sellers to note that this generally increases the length of the process and can reduce the sale price.

To demonstrate an example of when this less than flexible seller situation ended successfully, I will discuss the owner of a small manufacturing/distribution company. Upon our first meeting, this seller didn't appear super motivated and communicated to us that he wanted a six to eight times multiple, all cash deal. The company's annual revenues were in the four to five million-dollar range, with seller's discretionary earnings of less than one million dollars. I walked away from the meeting thinking, *this guy isn't serious*. But I recognized the probability of selling the business for a very high price—it's a great business with an interesting niche, vast expansion capabilities, and high profitability.

After aggressively marketing the business, and I mean *aggressively*, we connected with a private equity firm that owned a platform business, in a sister space. The private equity firm had a serious interest in the company and made plans to cross-sell their products to each other's customers. The seller received an all-cash offer, slightly lower than his unrealistic expectation, but a FULL CASH OFFER with a transition period of 30 days! Furthermore, the seller had owned the real estate and the buyer entered into a long-term lease with the seller. It was a perfect match.

Conversely, when a seller is moderately flexible on the terms and conditions, is willing to accept an earn out of some type, a seller note, and so on, we have more leverage and are able to negotiate a higher sales price. We have multiple examples of this scenario wherein the buyer was willing to pay the purchase price, and in a lot of cases more than the purchase price, once interest on seller's notes were calculated into the equation.

Now that we've discussed the seller components, primarily flexibility, and how this can have a direct effect on the type of buyer we market the business to and moreover, a direct effect on the pool of buyers, we will elaborate on the buyer selection process.

As we mentioned, knowing and understanding the seller first is key in the buyer selection process. Once we are clear on the seller's expectations, we are able to strategically pinpoint buyers within our extensive buyer database. Our database contains global, national, regional, and local buyers. From private equity firms actively buying businesses in designated industries, to strategic buyers for industries such as manufacturing, healthcare/medical, distribution, business services, staffing, and so on. Again, based on seller expectations, we generate a prospective buyer list based on buyer/seller matching criteria. Once we have identified prospective buyers, we start the process of reaching out to them, one by one, via phone call, email, follow-up, U.S. mail, social media, etc.

We implore typical sales methodology to reach selected buyers. Furthermore, as we have relationships with private equity buyers, strategic buyers seeking a portfolio company or an add-on in a certain industry, family offices, or individual investors, we are able to directly connect with key decision makers at such firms. After pinpointing said buyers, we discreetly distribute marketing materials to some, and then monitor buyer interests through confidential discussions. It is a process that continues to yield successful, well above industry average, closing rates for Aberdeen Advisors.

The subsequent sections provide greater detail regarding identifying and attracting multiple, ideal buyers.

Finding Ideal Buyers

Ideal buyers are not just buyers, but *qualified* buyers that have a serious interest in a business such as yours. When looking for ideal buyers, we are looking for those in alignment with the seller's company culture and what the seller is really looking for in a buyer. The potential buyers we speak with must have the integrity to keep the information confidential; we want to make sure they're not competitors that are trying to steal trade secrets.

We have local, regional, national, and international buyers in our network who we market to through websites, through portals, and through direct contact. We contact them confidentially to gauge their interest. If they're interested, we get them to sign a confidentiality agreement and then they get the information packet.

A Google search is a great way to look and see what's going on in the industry. The Wall Street Journal is another great resource. You can also gain knowledge through industry newsletters, which will tell you what businesses have been sold in the industry, and for how much money.

Another strategy on finding buyers is to place a classified ad. If you're in the construction industry, this would be placed in a newsletter for construction companies like yours. You'd want to be specific enough to say, "$20 million in revenue, qualified buyers only, looking to sell," and then give your private cell phone number only. You wouldn't identify your company name, but anyone who called you would figure out who you are. Therefore, at that point the confidentiality would be broken, but it's a very effective strategy. Those ads can sometimes be pretty expensive, and sometimes not, but that is a great way to find buyers in your industry.

There is a number of criteria on what makes an ideal buyer. One is they need to have the financial wherewithal or capability to buy the business. That either means they need to have the down payment—the equity needed to be put down—and then have a good credit score so that a bank will lend them the rest of the money. They have to have financial strength, and they have to have business acumen. The bank is going to require business experience that is relative to the company for sale; if somebody is in the restaurant business and is trying to buy a heating and air conditioning company, the bank may have pause with that. However, that weakness can be made up if the management team of the seller is going to stay on.

You also need to look at the motivation of the buyer; is this person just a tire-kicker? Are they a competitor that isn't really interested in buying, but wants to figure out what your company is doing, who your employees are, who your customers are, etc.? You have to be very very careful with that.

Part of the process is an art, part of it is a science. The science part is due diligence—does the interested buyer have the equity and business experience? Is the business in the right location for their company? Is the business commercial or residential? If it's both and they're only interested in residential, they're not a fit for your business.

A lot of potential buyers can be filtered out before you even sign a non-disclosure, which is our preference. But there are other things that you can't really determine until the buyer gets into it and sees the management team, what the financials look like, etc. However, you can vet the financial qualifications at the front end, and that's extremely important.

Finding Multiple Buyers

As previously mentioned, what can really drive the sale price up is to find not just one ideal buyer, but multiple buyers. At Aberdeen, we are very fortunate because we have databases of thousands of people who are actively looking for businesses to buy from over a ten-year period.

If you're a do-it-yourself person and you're going to look for buyers on your own, the first step would be to determine if you are willing to sell to one of your competitors. Do you know a competitor that your business would be an ideal fit for? Ideal companies may be ones that are in the same business as you, but aren't in your community yet. Or, they're in the same market, but they sell a different product to the same type of customer—not a direct competitor, but a complement to your company.

I had a client who was approached by a competitor who said, "We could sell your products to our clients and we can sell your products to our clients." In other words, "We've now got more customers and a wider product line. We're willing to pay for that. I'll pay you more than just a true financial buyer would pay." This type of scenario can be a great opportunity for you.

You can call indirect competitors and tell them you're looking for a strategic alliance, and ask if they have any interest. If they are interested, get a confidentiality in place. The problem with this strategy is that when you call them, they know who you are; that's one of the drawbacks of the DIY approach. You could have your lawyer or CPA reach out to that potential buyer, but again, the cloak of confidentiality is off, which is usually a huge drawback for people who want to sell their business. If you go through an intermediary like Aberdeen, they don't know which company is being sold.

Another way to find multiple buyers is to place ads on the internet sites for selling a business. In the United States, the #1 site for selling businesses under $10 million in revenue is www.bizbuysell.com and their sister website www.bizquest.com. There are many others; there are merger networks and other websites where you can pay $39/month, for example, to place your ad on the site. I don't recommend this strategy for bigger businesses, but for the smaller ones, it is one way to generate buyers.

The other strategy is to go to tradeshows in your industry. Attendees are often people from other regions, who might be looking to expand in your area. You could also buy information from sources such as PitchBook and CapIQ. Dunn and Bradstreet is another option, although it's very expensive. They will give you information on who is buying what type of company. You can buy cheaper lists from InfoUSA, through which you can acquire a mailing list, telemarketing list, or email list of companies to contact.

Once you've identified ideal buyers, it's time to negotiate.

CHAPTER 12:
Phase IV – Negotiate

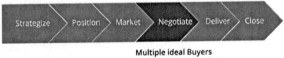
Being a successful business owner, I am certain you have employed your best negotiating skills on many occasions. Whether it was to land that dream client or to convince a superstar employee to stay with your company despite

receiving an incredible offer from a competitor, you have had to negotiate. You have had to deal or bargain with others, likely in your personal and professional life.

When it comes to transitioning your business, the negotiation of the sale of your business will prove to be one of the most important negotiations of your entire life. Trust me, you want a strong negotiator on your side of the transaction.

There are many factors which contribute to the negotiation process including, but not limited to, the number of prospective buyers interested in your company, the type of buyer(s) interested in the company, the buyers' motivation, your personal motivation, your plans once the business is sold, and your financial expectations.

Let's begin by addressing the points involving the prospective buyer(s). First, the number of interested buyers plays a huge role in how the negotiations will go. For example, if you have just one ideal buyer versus having multiple ideal buyers, your position of strength is greatly reduced. Secondly, the type of buyer is significant. Private equity buyers and strategic buyers offer sellers many different options.

Traditionally, though not always the case, private equity buyers are known for trading deals at lower multiples. They may also prefer an owner stay involved in the day-to-day operations. A strategic buyer or a competitor, driven by market share motivation, may actually offer the seller a higher multiple; a strategic buyer is also oftentimes able to capitalize on synergies of employees, vendor relationships, and client relationships which ultimately can result in increased sales and a decrease in expenses hence, higher profit margins. And, a strategic buyer may actually prefer that the owner not stay in the business after an agreed upon transition period.

In regards to the seller's position and how that can guide the negotiation process, a seller's motivation is the key component to the negotiation. If a seller is highly motivated to sell the business and highly motivated to exit the business, the conversation may be different than in the case wherein the seller actually wants a liquidity event but prefers to stay onboard for three to five years. Oftentimes, it is difficult for buyers and sellers but foremost, for sellers, to keep the discussions about the issues and not take the negotiations personally.

Once the offers or letters of intent have been submitted, the negotiations commence. This is the part I get excited about. I love negotiating and moving buyers towards stronger offers.

Let's explore in more detail an example of the negotiation process and how it transpired with one Aberdeen client. Our client was a successful multi-state distribution company with a unique niche. Our seller wanted a really high multiple given the size of the company and its cash flow. Our seller also wanted all cash and wanted to walk away from the company upon the sale. Our firm debated internally whether we should take on this client but ultimately, we really liked the seller and the company. Plus, the company was solidly put together with clean financials so we knew the company could withstand the due diligence process.

We told the seller, "We will work with you, but that's a pretty high multiple. We're not sure we're going to get all cash; it's not likely to be as easy as you think it is."

After much discussion on our strategy to market the company, we concluded the only real choice was a strategic buyer. Then, we were charged with the task of determining what strategic buyers may be interested and moreover, which could afford to pay such a multiple as the seller expected. We conducted a lot of research, purchased advertising on appropriate sites, and purchased very classified industry data which allowed us to identify approximately twenty strategic buyers within the industry that would be willing (and able) to pay the kind of multiple our seller had mandated.

This very laser-focused buyer data included some direct competitors, some broader industry competitors, and some buyers who weren't competitors per se, but offered complementary products. We approached the identified prospective buyers and five of the twenty expressed serious interest.

Out of those five, we received three indications of interest—a non-binding, prior to due diligence rough idea of value. With this, the buyer says in writing, "Will pay 5x cash flow for this type of business based on what we know now," which was the company name, historical financials, what they were selling, and what the management team looked like. Among those three buyers, the offers we received were significantly lower than what our seller wanted, but in line with what we advised for his company. From there, we were able to create a competitive bidding situation; two of the three buyers increased their offers with more cash, and one really stepped up and ultimately signed a strong letter of intent for an amount significantly higher than originally presented.

We closed on that offer, and our client was really pleased because it was all cash. He wanted a higher multiple, but it was a high multiple for his business. It's not all just about purchase price; creating a competitive bidding situation allows you to negotiate everything from the time on the due diligence, the time to closing, the amount of cash, and some of the other terms and conditions, such as how long the seller will stay on, how long the non-compete is for, etc. There are a lot of terms and conditions, and every seller is going to have different hot buttons, same with every buyer. The idea is to negotiate the best situation for you, the seller.

I would advise, if you decide to undertake the sales process without an M & A advisor, that you hire an exceptional M & A attorney and an experienced CPA to help you negotiate the terms. An attorney is well-versed with terms such as reps and warranties, due diligence, indemnification, non-compete, and all those details in which most sellers don't have industry knowledge.

A professional will especially come in handy for what's coming in the next phase, which can be excruciating: due diligence.

To wrap up this chapter, I will leave you with a few universal negotiating tips:

1) To the best of your ability, leave your ego out of the equation.

2) Try and stay focused on the issue at hand versus making the discussion point about yourself.

3) Always show respect for the other party; this goes a long way towards minimizing any hostility and will help both parties reach an agreement or a compromise sooner.

4) Be up front and don't be afraid to put any concerns you have front and center; this goes a long way towards creating goodwill and minimizing hostility.

5) Document the process in writing.

CHAPTER 13:
Phase V – Deliver

At this phase, you've negotiated the offer, you've gotten the offer, you've signed the letter of intent; and now you're in due diligence. This phase typically takes 60 to 120 days.

Again, during this critical process, approximately half of all deals fall apart. It is probably the most frustrating part of the process for the seller, and in some cases the buyer too. For the seller it is a nightmare; you get the 180 questions, and you need to answer them thoroughly and accurately. Most of the business owners we work with are running the business, and they don't want their employees to know they're trying to sell. They're not convinced they're going to close, so they don't want their employees to know. However, in most cases they need to get their chief financial officer, their accounting person, their bookkeeper, and their human resources person involved in the process, to help them get the information they need. They're definitely going to have to get their lawyer and CPA involved, and that's going to require their time, their money, and a lot of their energy.

The duration of due diligence is generally spelled out in the contract or letter of intent. As the seller, you have to deliver the documents required in a timely manner. You need a qualified, experienced deal maker on your side to properly document your due diligence.

This is when the deal will either go south or be re-traded on price. For example, if the seller gets into due diligence and didn't know that 60% of the revenue comes from three customers, the seller will almost immediately re-trade the deal or say they're not going to buy it. What we try to do with our clients is to be very front-end driven. We don't want the buyer surprised by any particular weakness. There's no reason, in our opinion, to sign a letter of intent and then turn around in due diligence and say, "Oh by the way, we have a big environmental problem." We would rather address that on the front end, get the parties to agree with the next steps, and factor that into the price of the deal. The due diligence phase would simply confirm what we had already told them.

Top Tips to Survive Due Diligence

1. **Be very front-end driven.** We want to be on solid ground from the beginning of the process, to the end. If we're not on solid ground, we want to have an answer for it. We never want to be surprised, and we never want our buyer to be surprised. We like clients that understand and appreciate how important this step is, because there's a lot of liability in selling a company.

2. **Get your team involved early.** Get your key team members involved early, so that they have time to put the information together. This includes your lawyer, your CPA, and your CFO. Get the information you need from them up front and in the Cloud.

3. **Be patient.** It's going to be challenging. It's going to be a grind. There are going to be a million reasons

for you to sack the deal. That is probably your impatience speaking.

4. **Sell when things are going well.** You don't want your ideal buyer to say, "Hey, you got a worker's comp claim. Your insurance is going up. You lost a big client. Your backlog is going down." You want to be selling when your business is on the uptrend and things are going well. You do not want to be selling when things are starting to plateau off or head down.

The Due Diligence Nightmare

I received a due diligence list from a potential buyer and forwarded it to my client. He calls me and asks, "Which of these do I have to answer?" I said, "You have to answer them all." He said, "Ten years of tax returns?" In some cases, yes—ten years of tax returns. And in all cases— you must answer all of the questions.

One section may be in regards to human resources. "I want every employment contract. I want every insurance policy. I want every participant and all of the 401(k) plan documents." Then there's the legal section. Then operations. Then financial. Each of them with their own litany of detailed list of questions and requirements.

Then the potential buyer has his own due diligence. He's going to send in his company's CPA firm to do a financial audit. Then he's going to send in his law firm to do a legal audit. Then he's going to send his environmental firm in to do an environmental study on the real estate. Then his HR people, his insurance people…the buyer is going to uncover literally everything.

The process can be incredibly overwhelming for the seller, which is why it's good to work with an M&A firm. Our role is to manage both the seller and the buyer. The buyers may ask for information or access that they aren't entitled to as this stage of the process. For example, they may want to see all of your customer names right now. However, it's way too early in the due diligence process to provide that information. We tell them they have to wait. They'll say, "We want to meet with all the key employees." We tell them, "No. You're not going to meet with the key employees until the very end, if at all." We negotiate this process for you.

There are some situations where the seller has to acquiesce. For example, I represented a client whose potential buyer—a private equity fund—said, "You have 80% of your revenue with this one customer. We are not buying your business without meeting that customer." My seller, who was 82 years old, was going crazy. He said, "There's no way." I said, "Hank, if you lose this one customer, you literally have no business. The buyer needs to meet this customer." He was mad. He was afraid to tell his customer that he was selling the business; he might lose the customer's business, or he might lose his employees once the word got out. But he finally agreed.

Before that meeting, the representative from the equity fund said, "Here's how the meeting's going to go. Hank's going to introduce his client. Then you're going to follow my lead. This is what you're going to say." Sometimes the seller has their own system and agenda; they know that people are going to get scared, and that confidentiality is critical. When we met with the customer in this case, she was great. She said, "You're 80 years old. Of course you're going to sell the business."

Sometimes, the seller is really caught off guard with what the buyer is asking for; they are faced with needing to provide documents that they never thought they would need. The buyer may ask, "Where are your Articles of Incorporation?" or "Here are your major supplier contracts, but nobody has a signed copy." In some cases, the business owner may have been doing business with those suppliers for ten years; they will say, "I never thought that would be an issue." But they need to get those contracts signed in order to sell the business.

There are numerous contracts the seller will need to have ready. We represented a lawn care company that was on several different properties. If the owner sells the company and there's an environmental issue, it's going to be the new buyer's issue. Environmental problems and liability can be mega dollars, and the buyer knew that. The seller had never done an environmental study. Now, they needed to have one done in order to sell.

Virtual Data Rooms

In the old days, everything was done on paper; there were data rooms, stuffed with big binders of papers, file cabinets, copies upon copies. Now, when we work with clients, we set up virtual data rooms which house all of the due diligence requests. If there are 180 items that are requested for due diligence, we would put that information up in a very secure, password-protected, cloud-based system that the buyer's counsel, buyer's CPA, and the buyer can access.

For example, there will be a human resources section, which will have payroll information, 401(k) information, employee benefit information, and medical policies. Each due diligence item will have a folder, and we will put that data in there.

The reason we're so front-end driven is because an enormous amount of information is required for this process. It is going to tie up your accountant, your CPA, your lawyer, your key internal people. We want to get as much information organized and in the data room at the very beginning of the process, so that when we get an offer and accept that offer, we can get it closed.

Sample Due Diligence Request

See appendix for due diligence request list.

CHAPTER 14:
Phase VI – Close

ABERDEEN'S "SIX STEPS TO SOLD"

The six-step proprietary process that's helped us close hundreds of transactions

Deliver   Close

Serious Results for Serious Sellers.

Take a deep breath – you're now (almost) officially free to pursue whatever goal brought you to the selling table in the first place.

The closing is both the most exciting and also most anxious part of the process. You can be days, or maybe weeks away from the closing date, and what typically happens is the buyer's bank needs a document. Then they need another document. Then the bank's lawyer needs four days to review the closing documents. You had set the closing date for the middle of the month, and now it's the end of the month and the document requests keep coming.

You're very frustrated. Now, some of your employees know you are selling, and maybe even some of your customers. Things are feeling a little out of your control; you're also not even completely sure if the deal is going to close. Or, you're not fully accepting that it's going to happen.

Just Hang in There

Generally, at this stage the close will happen—the due diligence is done, everybody's committed to the process. However, deals do blow up at the eleventh hour for sometimes silly little things, because your emotions are so frayed by that point.

Just hang in there. It may take a day. It may take a week. It may take a month. We will ultimately get it closed.

Many times we've had our our clients want to blow the deal up at the very end; they felt like they were getting nickeled and dimed and that the bank was being unreasonable. Unfortunately, in most cases that's just part of the process.

You will sign hundreds, sometimes even thousands of pages of reps, of warranties, of indemnifications. Hopefully you've had a good lawyer that is an expert M&A lawyer who has walked you through all the documents. Hopefully, you have a good CPA who has helped you minimize taxes. Hopefully you have an estate planner that might have put part of your company in a trust, so that you can minimize taxes. If you've done all of that properly, then you go to the closing table well prepared to get the most amount of money and the least amount of risk.

What is Most Likely to Kill a Deal

Emotions and ego are the factors most likely to kill a deal at this stage. Sellers get frustrated that the process is not going as fast as they thought it would. It hasn't been as easy as they thought it would be. In some cases, the seller is offended by some of the questions. Now, banks and CPA firms and buyers are requiring a background check and a credit check on the seller. You have to fill out IRS Form 4506 to verify your tax return. That can be very insulting to a business owner that's very prideful that they do everything correctly.

The seller is burnt out at this point; they are getting asked thousands of questions, many of which are repeat questions that the seller feels like he has answered several times. The bank wants this, the CPA firm wants that, the lawyer wants this. The seller gets very frustrated and angry that things aren't going his way, he feels a loss of control and all of a sudden he has a temper tantrum and the deal blows off when it shouldn't have. Or a lot of times, the buyer and seller want to do the deal, but the attorneys go at it. That kills deals as well.

The day before closing, one of my clients and his wife went ballistic. My job was to "get them off the ledge before they jumped." A lot of times, if the clients were going through the process by themselves, they would blow the deal up. Instead, I am there to tell them, "I know. I understand. It's a nightmare. Remember what you said. You wanted to transition out so you could spend time with your grandkids." I try to get them focused back on their motivation.

To keep from having an outburst and potentially creating a disaster, you need to refer back to your motivation. Why are you doing this? Is it to take care of your retirement? To take care of your grandkids? Is it to give money to your church or school? Is it because your health is declining, because you're working too hard? Do you want to travel? Don't blow off a deal when you're in the ten-yard line. It may be ten hard, painful yards, but you're about to get this business sold. You have to keep the end game in mind.

That's why it's so important to be really motivated and clear on your goal from the beginning. This is going to be a hard process. We do the heavy lifting, but you've got to pay your CPA, pay your lawyer, and get your internal staff to go through thousands of documents.

Here is a sample guide for what needs to be prepared for the closing:

Closing Documents: (Sample Closing Checklist)

ASSET or STOCK SALE

Closing checklist

Buyer ("b"):	Name address
Seller ("s"):	Name address
Lender ("l"):	Name & contact info
Closing agent/:	Name, contact info, address
Buyer's counsel ("bc"):	Name, contact info, address
Seller's counsel ("bc"):	Name, contact info, address
Lender's counsel ("lc"):	Name, contact info, address:
Broker	Name, contact info, address
Sale price:	$_____
Re:	Sale of 1,000 shares (all outstanding shares) or 100% of assets of company name
Closing date:	
Status key:	R – received; a – approved; w – waived; d – drafted

Closing Documents:

1. Assignment of Shares (if applicable)

2. Original Stock Certificates (if applicable) – Endorsed and Blank

3. Closing Certificate - Seller

4. Closing Certificate - Buyer

5. Employment Agreement (attached to Contract)

6. Copy of Lease

7. Resignation of Officers & Directors

8. Non-Compete / Non-Solicitation Agreement

9. Disclosure and Acknowledgment of Non - Representation

10. Further Assurance and Compliance Agreement

11. Bill of Sale – Transfer of equipment from Seller Co. to Buyer Co.

12. Broker Hold Harmless Agreement

13. Buyer's Assurance Certificate

14. Seller's Assurance Certificate

15. Settlement Statement

Organizational / Trust Documents

16. Buyer – _____.

    (a) Copy of Articles of Incorporation & amendments

    (b) Copy of ByLaws & amendments

    (c) Resolution & Incumbency Certificate

17. Seller – Trust Documents

    (a) Copy of Trust Docs & Certificate of Trust

18. Seller - _____.

    (a) Copy of Articles of Incorporation & Amendments

    (b) Copy of ByLaws & Amendments

Chapter 15:

Transition: After the Sale

After the close is official and you've received your money...
you have turned your blood, sweat, and tears into cash. Congratulations! This is a very exciting time, but it can also be somewhat confusing.

You're about to go through a transition phase. You will wonder, "Am I really closed? Is anything really different?" Everybody is congratulating you, but it still hasn't sunk in.

We warn clients up front that—especially if they're the founder—they are going to go through the seven stages of grief. These are:

1) shock and disbelief
2) denial
3) bargaining
4) guilt
5) anger

6) depression, and then

7) acceptance, or hope.

Again, hang in there.

Remember your motivation? The greener pastures on the other side? You now have the freedom and ability to travel, the ability to pay off any debts, to be debt-free and footloose.

The transition is usually really hard for a lot of our sellers who stay on in the business after the sale, because they're used to making the decisions. They're not used to reporting to anybody. Now, this 35-year-old is in there making changes that you don't agree with. Or, he's doing a great job, but doing it differently than you did—he's creating a website, whereas you never had one before. He's putting things in the Cloud. Or they're trying things you've already tried and you know they don't work. It can be very humbling.

The transition presents quite the emotional ride, especially for male sellers; it's hard for women, too, but it seems that men's egos are more tied to their businesses. That business is their identity. For decades, they've said, "This is what I do. I'm the trucking guy, or I'm the manufacturing of widgets guy…and now where is my identity?"

I often hear from clients, "I don't want to play golf every day." Or they say, "My wife does not want me at the house full-time." For the wives of business owners who have usually been on location all day, all of a sudden, the home goes from being their kingdom to feeling like it's no longer theirs. That can cause some friction.

Business owners are usually type As, who get bored quick. A lot of sellers deal with these issues by buying a small business, or doing volunteer work. I talked to one of my clients recently, who is only six months into the transition after selling his business, and he wants to buy a small business. He needs something else to do.

One client, Mike Charles at CGM, sold his business, then stayed on for a year and a half, under one condition: "I'm going to be the Grand Poobah still." It was tough, but we found the right buyer for him. Now, he's moved on from that company, but he's building a storage unit business. It's a really easy business to run, which means he can also go and travel with his wife Darlene around the world. He got what he wanted. Darlene got what she wanted.

I asked him if I could use him as a reference. He said, "You can use me. You can say I'm the happiest contractor in America. Quote, Mike Charles." I said, "That's perfect. You just made my day, Mike."

That's what I want for you, too. I want you to be the happiest business seller in America. You've earned your freedom. You've built your business. It's time for your reward.

CONCLUSION

Now that you've completed this book, you are far more informed and prepared for selling your business than the average business owner. You have learned the most common pitfalls to selling a business—namely not having an exit strategy in place, and waiting until it's too late. You have determined your motivation, the driving force that will keep you committed to closing the deal when the going gets tough.

As you read this book, your expectations for your business valuation have likely become more realistic, and you gained a clearer picture of the complexities of the M&A process. You understand how important it is to start early, and to assemble a team of professionals that will help you get the best buyer, the best offer, and the biggest payout. These professionals should include a lawyer and a CPA—both specialized in mergers and acquisitions—and, if you really want the highest chance at achieving the result of your dreams with the least amount of headache, an M&A advisor.

We have outlined the highly successful six-step process that we at Aberdeen undergo with each of our clients; we help strategize, position, market, negotiate, deliver, and close the deal—so that you can focus on keeping your business going strong during this critical period of transition.

I hope you've gotten a lot of value out of this book. My intention in writing it was to have you begin to ask questions about what it will take to sell your business. Now that you know what's possible, what are you going to do about it? How can you get started down the path to turning your blood, sweat and tears into cash?

First of all, don't get stuck doing nothing. If you haven't prepared your business for exit, it may seem like you have a long way to climb out of financial and paperwork muck. That may be true—but the sooner you get started, and the sooner you enlist the help of your staff and professionals, the smoother the process will be in the long-run and the greater your reward will be. Once you're debt-free, traveling the world with your wife, or watching your grandkids grow, you'll hopefully forget all about the stress of the process and just enjoy the outcome.

Don't just take my word for it, ask any of Aberdeen's former clients, such as Dr. Mitch Lowenstein.

A friend of Dr. Lowenstein saw my keynote speech at a dental conference and referred him to me. Mitch called me and said, "I'd love to get together and discuss working with you." We met for lunch at Panera Bread. He had a very successful medical practice; he was a top rheumatologist in Florida, and he wasn't even sure he could sell his business because he was the key doctor. After digging in with him, however, I thought I could get quite a bit of money for it. We made an agreement to work together, and six months later we sold it.

A nice lady bought his practice, and afterward we met again at a different Panera Bread. He literally started crying, telling me he was so happy that this woman was buying his practice, and that his doctors and staff were going to have a job. He loved his employees. He really didn't need the money from the sale; it was more about keeping what he had built going, having a job for his employees, and taking care of his patients.

Working with people like Dr. Lowenstein is what keeps me passionate. We've seen a person get cancer or have a car wreck and we've watched their business go down really quickly. It's nice to be a part of a success story like Dr. Lowenstein's. It's why I do what I do.

If you've made it to the end of this book then perhaps you have begun to seriously consider selling your business to create a secure future for yourself, your family, and your employees… to get the freedom you've always desired; to travel, to volunteer, to finally spend time with the grandkids like you had always planned.

If you're realizing there is a lot to selling a business and that you need help, please call me confidentially at (727) 639-4716. I am happy to discuss how I can guide you to freedom. For more information and free resources and white-papers, visit our website at: **www.aberdeenadvisors.com**

Welcome to the rest of your life. If you take all the steps outlined in this book, it really will be as good as you imagined.

Appendix

DUE DILIGENCE REQUEST LIST for ABC Company

The requested items and disclosures should be made with respect to the company being purchased (the "Company") and its business and assets. The requested items and disclosures are intended to cover all material and relevant aspects of the Company for the purpose of evaluating the proposed transaction. Thus, if you withhold any item, document, disclosure or other information requested below on the basis that you believe it is non-material, irrelevant or otherwise, please provide a statement identifying such information being withheld. Accordingly, we urge you to err by being over-responsive than to omit any item or information which might prove to be material or relevant to the contemplated transaction.

In responding to this request, please confirm (i) which items are not applicable or to which your response is "None," and (ii) that you have provided us with all existing documents under each item. Please organize the due diligence materials in accordance with the below section numbers and provide consolidated responses to queries and electronic versions of documents in .pdf format, along with a copy of this request list with the appropriate status boxes marked to:

First Name, Last Name: [Insert Buyer Info]
Contact info:

To the extent any of the items listed below are amended, updated, or supplemented and/or new items are created, entered into, or received during the period in which we are completing the due diligence process and finalizing the transaction documents, please promptly provide us with the amendments, updates, supplements, or new items.

Ref	ITEM DESCRIPTION	Previously Provided	Provided With List	To be Provided	None	Not Applicable
	CORPORATE MATTERS					
	Organization and Good Standing:					
1	Copies of the Certificate of Incorporation, By-laws, Articles of Organization, Operating Agreement and other organizational documents, as amended and as currently in effect	☐	☐	☐	☐	☐

Ref	ITEM DESCRIPTION	Previously Provided	Provided With List	To be Provided	None	Not Applicable
2	Certificate of good standing (including payment of taxes) and/or certificates of qualifications from appropriate authorities from the state of incorporation of the Company and the state(s) in which the Company is qualified to do business	☐	☐	☐	☐	☐
3	A description of all material inter-company products/services provided to or on behalf of the Company by any of its affiliates and the costs associated therewith, together with a list of all material assets, tangible and intangible, that are used by the Company but owned by any of its affiliates	☐	☐	☐	☐	☐
4	A list of all corporate names, fictitious names and assumed names used by the Company now or at any time within the past 5 years and copies of registrations	☐	☐	☐	☐	☐
Regulatory Matters:						
5	List and copies of all notices, information requests, permits, licenses, registrations, franchises, variances, approvals and certificates of authority from foreign, federal, state, governmental and local authorities including any municipal or regional airport authority held or required to be held	☐	☐	☐	☐	☐

Ref	ITEM DESCRIPTION	Previously Provided	Provided With List	To be Provided	None	Not Applicable
6	Description of any allegation or claim (including copies of any claims made in writing), made within the past three years, that the Company has acted in violation of any law, regulation, ordinance, or other requirement of any governmental authority, including, but not limited to, OSHA, EPA, EEOC, antitrust, zoning, taxation and environmental agencies	☐	☐	☐	☐	☐
7	Copies of all reports and statements filed with, any correspondence with, and any transcripts of any significant proceedings before, any state, federal or other governmental regulatory agencies within the past three years	☐	☐	☐	☐	☐
8	Copies of any regulatory (assistance, supervisory or other) agreements which relate to the operation of the Company	☐	☐	☐	☐	☐
9	Copies of reports of examination or review, and any related correspondence, of the Company's operations by state, federal or other governmental authorities for the past three years	☐	☐	☐	☐	☐
Contracts and Commitments:						
10	Copies of all standard forms for customer sales, service and supply contracts/orders	☐	☐	☐	☐	☐

Ref	ITEM DESCRIPTION	Previously Provided	Provided With List	To be Provided	None	Not Applicable
11	Details of all customer warranties, indemnities or guarantees in existence	☐	☐	☐	☐	☐
12	Details of agency agreements in place or under negotiation	☐	☐	☐	☐	☐
13	Copies of all supplier contracts/orders/ service agreements where annual purchases exceed $5,000	☐	☐	☐	☐	☐
14	Details of specific supplier pricing and discount arrangements	☐	☐	☐	☐	☐
15	Brief description of contracts subject to renegotiations or extensions to contracts that are subject to the exercise of an option	☐	☐	☐	☐	☐
16	Copies of all agreements with governmental agencies involving the payment of more than $10,000 in the aggregate	☐	☐	☐	☐	☐
18	Details of any other material matters including copies of any agreements not provided in response to any other question which cannot be terminated by the Company on thirty days months' notice or less without payment of compensation or any special fees	☐	☐	☐	☐	☐
19	Copies of all agreements involving the payment of commissions or other consideration or discounts with respect to the conduct of the business of the Company	☐	☐	☐	☐	☐

Ref	ITEM DESCRIPTION	Previously Provided	Provided With List	To be Provided	None	Not Applicable
20	Description of any facts and/or circumstances which may give rise to the cancellation or termination of or claim for damages or loss under, any of the agreements, arrangements, or understandings referred to herein	☐	☐	☐	☐	☐
21	Copies of any Airport Development Plans	☐	☐	☐	☐	☐
22	Please provide details (with copy documentation where appropriate) of any grant or other financial assistance received or applied for by the Company from any governmental or regulatory authority or body	☐	☐	☐	☐	☐
23	List of all hangar and tie-down tenants with monthly rental rate, and copies of all leases/contracts of tenants, if any	☐	☐	☐	☐	☐
24	Copy of credit policy	☐	☐	☐	☐	☐
25	Copies of all employment, consulting, nondisclosure, non-solicitation or non-competition agreements between the Company and any of its employees or any third party.	☐	☐	☐	☐	☐
26	Contracts with officers, directors, shareholders, or related organizations.	☐	☐	☐	☐	☐
27	Consulting, billing and management agreements.	☐	☐	☐	☐	☐
28	Office equipment leases (data processing, telephone, facsimile, postal meters, computers, etc.)	☐	☐	☐	☐	☐

Ref	ITEM DESCRIPTION	Previously Provided	Provided With List	To be Provided	None	Not Applicable
29	Service and maintenance agreements.	☐	☐	☐	☐	☐
30	Copies of any collective bargaining agreements.	☐	☐	☐	☐	☐
31	Copies of all loan, credit and security agreements, including any mortgages or other security documents that encumber any of the assets to be acquired.	☐	☐	☐	☐	☐
32	Copies of all construction contracts	☐	☐	☐	☐	☐
33	Copies of all brokerage, finders or similar agreements	☐	☐	☐	☐	☐
	Litigation/Investigations					
34	Complete list of and documents concerning any pending or threatened litigation, administrative or arbitration proceeding, or government claim and documents regarding material claims settled or adjudicated within the past 5 years for the Company (including nature of the claim, amount involved, and status of the proceedings)	☐	☐	☐	☐	☐
35	Documents relating to any pending or threatened investigations or proceedings by any governmental agencies (including environmental and employee safety matters) with respect to the Company and documents regarding material claims settled or adjudicated within the past 5 years	☐	☐	☐	☐	☐

Ref	ITEM DESCRIPTION	Previously Provided	Provided With List	To be Provided	None	Not Applicable
36	List of any significant legal problems or issues now affecting or which are likely to affect the Company in the future.	☐	☐	☐	☐	☐
37	Documents with respect to pending or threatened material labor disputes (including strikes, grievances and arbitration proceedings)	☐	☐	☐	☐	☐
38	Documents regarding any material contingent liabilities and material asserted or unasserted claims and information regarding any asserted or unasserted violation of any employee safety and environmental laws and any asserted or unasserted pollution clean-up liability (including any environmental surveys and reports prepared by internal personnel or outside consultants)	☐	☐	☐	☐	☐
39	All consent decrees, judgments, other decrees or orders, settlement agreements and other agreements within the past three years, including any such decrees, judgments, orders or agreements relating to environmental matters	☐	☐	☐	☐	☐
CONSENTS/APPROVALS						
40	List of all contracts, governmental permits, leases and licenses that will require the consent of a third party to the transaction or to continued effectiveness of such contract, permit, lease or license after the closing.	☐	☐	☐	☐	☐

Ref	ITEM DESCRIPTION	Previously Provided	Provided With List	To be Provided	None	Not Applicable
41	List necessary consents from lenders and/or issuing authorities to sell the assets of the Company	☐	☐	☐	☐	☐
42	A description of the Company's understanding of the approval process and timelines thereof for each of the above referenced agreements requiring consent	☐	☐	☐	☐	☐
INTELLECTUAL PROPERTY						
43	A list and summary of any intellectual property or intangible assets owned or used by the Company, with a notation of whether each is registered or unregistered.	☐	☐	☐	☐	☐
44	A list of the Company's websites and domain names with confirmation of who owns the sites and any agreements relating to the development and maintenance of the sites	☐	☐	☐	☐	☐
45	Any assignments, exclusive licenses or other encumbrances (including liens or mortgages) related to intellectual property of the Company	☐	☐	☐	☐	☐
46	License, sponsorship or user agreements under which any third party is permitted to use intellectual property rights of the Company	☐	☐	☐	☐	☐

Ref	ITEM DESCRIPTION	Previously Provided	Provided With List	To be Provided	None	Not Applicable
47	License, sponsorship or user agreements under which the Company is permitted to use intellectual property rights owned by a third party, including details of any royalty or other payments made to a third party by the Company in the last three years	☐	☐	☐	☐	☐
	MARKETING					
48	Website contacts for hosting, access to change domain ownership and server residence	☐	☐	☐	☐	☐
49	Electronic logo and art files, high resolution images and photos as used for marketing purposes	☐	☐	☐	☐	☐
50	Video files if any	☐	☐	☐	☐	☐
51	Photos of facilities both interior and exterior	☐	☐	☐	☐	☐
	REVENUE MGMT/SALES					
52	List of major customers (by name and by tail) showing gallons and MPG for prior year. Please note special pricing and provide copies of written fuel price agreements, if any	☐	☐	☐	☐	☐
53	List of tenants (including tail numbers) including expiration of tenant agreement	☐	☐	☐	☐	☐
55	Property management revenue for prior year, by tenant	☐	☐	☐	☐	☐

Ref	ITEM DESCRIPTION	Previously Provided	Provided With List	To be Provided	None	Not Applicable
56	Gallons and fuel margin per gallon by tenant for current and prior year, including copies of written fuel price agreements, if any	☐	☐	☐	☐	☐
57	List of tenant tail numbers (at least the major ones)	☐	☐	☐	☐	☐
58	List of any other tail numbers that might be "unavailable" market; for example, are there any corporate fuel farms on the airport?	☐	☐	☐	☐	☐
59	Retail JetA and Avgas posted price for Company and competitor(s) along with information regarding whether or not relative price position has changed over the last 2-3 years	☐	☐	☐	☐	☐
	RISK MANAGEMENT					
60	Insurance claims history for the past 5 years (including products liability claims) and a description of any self-insurance programs and any retro-premium obligations	☐	☐	☐	☐	☐
61	For the past five (5) years, provide a summary of all insurance policies including insurer, type of cover, amounts insured, premiums payable, main endorsements, deductibles and renewal dates, taken out by or on behalf of the Target, or in which they participate (e.g. Group policies)	☐	☐	☐	☐	☐

Ref	ITEM DESCRIPTION	Previously Provided	Provided With List	To be Provided	None	Not Applicable
62	Details of:					
	All paid and outstanding insurance claims (*) (including employment disputes/sexual harassment)	☐	☐	☐	☐	☐
	Details of all paid/outstanding claims which exceed $100,000 in the past five years	☐	☐	☐	☐	☐
	Description of all currently outstanding claims where reserve or claimed amount exceeds $75,000	☐	☐	☐	☐	☐
63	Details of current or past Regulatory actions, Prosecutions, Sanctions, Outstanding litigation	☐	☐	☐	☐	☐
64	Copies and description of all surety bonds including amounts, premiums, dates and sureties	☐	☐	☐	☐	☐
65	Copies of all key person life insurance policies relating to any person employed	☐	☐	☐	☐	☐
66	Copies and description of directors and officers indemnification and reimbursement policy	☐	☐	☐	☐	☐
67	Details of any dispute with any insurer or anything that the Company is aware of that may invalidate a policy	☐	☐	☐	☐	☐
68	Details of any exposure to EPA/Superfund liability	☐	☐	☐	☐	☐

Ref	ITEM DESCRIPTION	Previously Provided	Provided With List	To be Provided	None	Not Applicable
69	Record of all workplace injuries over the last three years	☐	☐	☐	☐	☐
70	Details of all foreign exchange cover eg. hedging	☐	☐	☐	☐	☐
71	Details of internal audits	☐	☐	☐	☐	☐
EMPLOYEES, COMPENSATION & BENEFITS						
Employees:						
72	Organization charts for the business by departments	☐	☐	☐	☐	☐
73	Headcount by department, job title, PT or FT, exempt and non-exempt	☐	☐	☐	☐	☐
74	Details of succession plans, identifying key individuals with potential	☐	☐	☐	☐	☐
75	CV's of all senior management personnel and key employees	☐	☐	☐	☐	☐
76	Listing of all employees showing: Job titles, job description, department, length of service, gender, race, current compensation (rate of pay and bonus) and other benefits, date/amount of last increase, exempt/non-exempt status, union representation, date of birth, severance conditions, on FMLA (Y/N).	☐	☐	☐	☐	☐
77	Job Description for all positions	☐	☐	☐	☐	☐

Ref	ITEM DESCRIPTION	Previously Provided	Provided With List	To be Provided	None	Not Applicable
78	List of all employees of the Company who are not citizens of the United States and who are not permanent residents of the United States, together with a listing of each such employee's visa status and visa expiration date	☐	☐	☐	☐	☐
79	Details of staff turnover and details any key personnel losses over last 2 yrs (*)	☐	☐	☐	☐	☐
80	Turnover statistics for past three years	☐	☐	☐	☐	☐
81	Copy of employee attitude survey or any other employee survey e.g. internal customer	☐	☐	☐	☐	☐
82	Details of management/employee appraisal arrangements and procedures in place to identify training and development needs.	☐	☐	☐	☐	☐
83	Training and development programs	☐	☐	☐	☐	☐
Policies and Procedures						
84	Copy of Employee handbook or equivalent, company policies and procedures, work rules	☐	☐	☐	☐	☐
85	Disciplinary action process	☐	☐	☐	☐	☐
86	Travel/entertainment policies	☐	☐	☐	☐	☐
87	Promotion policy	☐	☐	☐	☐	☐
Employee Contracts						
88	Copy of standard employment contracts / offer letters.	☐	☐	☐	☐	☐

Ref	ITEM DESCRIPTION	Previously Provided	Provided With List	To be Provided	None	Not Applicable
89	Copies of all employment contracts, non-compete agreements, confidentiality agreements or other agreements not on standard terms and conditions.	☐	☐	☐	☐	☐
90	Description and copies of all "golden parachutes" or other termination/severance agreements, plans or arrangements which provide for payments upon a change in control.	☐	☐	☐	☐	☐
Unemployment Claims						
91	State rates	☐	☐	☐	☐	☐
92	Number of recent claims	☐	☐	☐	☐	☐
93	Annual cost of unemployment insurance	☐	☐	☐	☐	☐
Compensation and Payroll						
94	Details of compensation administration - exempt, non-exempt and executives: Wage & Salary ranges, differentials (amount and reason), overtime, pay increase procedures to include frequency & percent of increase.	☐	☐	☐	☐	☐
95	Copies of all incentive and bonus programs	☐	☐	☐	☐	☐
96	Severance guidelines	☐	☐	☐	☐	☐
97	Commission arrangements	☐	☐	☐	☐	☐
98	Information on any grandfathered compensation, incentive or bonus programs	☐	☐	☐	☐	☐

Ref	ITEM DESCRIPTION	Previously Provided	Provided With List	To be Provided	None	Not Applicable
99	Details of any agreed wage/salary increases	☐	☐	☐	☐	☐
100	Details of all deferred compensation plans and arrangements	☐	☐	☐	☐	☐
101	Details of any special compensation commitments	☐	☐	☐	☐	☐
102	Annual payroll YTD and prior two years Year to date payroll records and prior year registers	☐	☐	☐	☐	☐
Benefits						
103	Copy health and safety manual / policies and procedures	☐	☐	☐	☐	☐
104	Details of all employee benefit schemes / SPD, plan documents, 5500 reports including:					
	(a) Life insurance	☐	☐	☐	☐	☐
	(b) AD & D insurance	☐	☐	☐	☐	☐
	(c) Medical insurance	☐	☐	☐	☐	☐
	(d) Dental insurance	☐	☐	☐	☐	☐
	(e) Vision insurance	☐	☐	☐	☐	☐
	(f) Flexible spending accounts – SPD, employee balances, etc.	☐	☐	☐	☐	☐
	(g) Retiree medical plans (participation and funding)	☐	☐	☐	☐	☐
	(h) Pensions etc.	☐	☐	☐	☐	☐

Ref	ITEM DESCRIPTION	Previously Provided	Provided With List	To be Provided	None	Not Applicable
	(i) 401K (include schedule of current invest options, investment statement, balances loan information and outstanding loans, copies of year-end testing, testing statements for past 5 years)	☐	☐	☐	☐	☐
	(j) Short Term Disability	☐	☐	☐	☐	☐
	(k) Long Term Disability	☐	☐	☐	☐	☐
105	Copies of any stock option plans, CSARs, phantom plans, restrictive stock plans.	☐	☐	☐	☐	☐
106	Paid Time off for employees: Vacation, sick leave, holidays, personal holidays, and personal leave.	☐	☐	☐	☐	☐
107	Leaves of absence	☐	☐	☐	☐	☐
108	Tuition reimbursement	☐	☐	☐	☐	☐
109	Company issued vehicles/car allowances	☐	☐	☐	☐	☐
110	Relocation policies	☐	☐	☐	☐	☐
111	Service awards	☐	☐	☐	☐	☐
112	Executive benefits	☐	☐	☐	☐	☐
113	List of all former employees and qualified family members currently receiving COBRA or state continuation coverage to include date of event, expiration of COBRA coverage.	☐	☐	☐	☐	☐
114	List of all employees receiving long or short term disability payments and description of any arrangements for salary continuance currently in place	☐	☐	☐	☐	☐

Ref	ITEM DESCRIPTION	Previously Provided	Provided With List	To be Provided	None	Not Applicable
115	Description of all other benefits, not included above, involving any present or former employee (e.g. automobiles, use of facilities by employees, matching contribution plans etc)	☐	☐	☐	☐	☐
116	Details of all retiree healthcare arrangements, liabilities, participation and funding – SPD and 5500	☐	☐	☐	☐	☐
117	Copies of administrative services contracts	☐	☐	☐	☐	☐
118	Information on any grandfather benefits	☐	☐	☐	☐	☐
119	Information on any other benefits offered to exempt, non-exempt or executive employees not listed above	☐	☐	☐	☐	☐
	Pension					
120	For each pension or other post retirement benefit plan or profit sharing or savings plan covering current or former company directors and/or employees, copies of:					
	(a) Plan document, including amendments (and a description of any changes in these plans proposed, agreed upon, or under consideration)	☐	☐	☐	☐	☐
	(b) Actuarial reports for each of the last three years (if applicable)	☐	☐	☐	☐	☐
	(c) Trust instruments	☐	☐	☐	☐	☐
	(d) Trust balance sheet, if any	☐	☐	☐	☐	☐
	(e) Summary plan descriptions	☐	☐	☐	☐	☐

Ref	ITEM DESCRIPTION	Previously Provided	Provided With List	To be Provided	None	Not Applicable
	(f) The latest application for determination to the Inland Revenue Service (IRS)	☐	☐	☐	☐	☐
	(g) Any IRS determination letter	☐	☐	☐	☐	☐
	(a) Any other IRS ruling relating to the plan	☐	☐	☐	☐	☐
	(h) The latest Annual Report on Form 550, 5500C or 5500K	☐	☐	☐	☐	☐
	(i) A schedule showing contributions made by or on behalf of the Company for each of the last five years	☐	☐	☐	☐	☐
	(j) Copies of all bonds required under ERISA 412	☐	☐	☐	☐	☐
	(k) Details of any special benefits for executives, directors or other employees	☐	☐	☐	☐	☐
	(l) Disclosure note for pensions and for other post-retirement benefits from the latest year's Company financial statements	☐	☐	☐	☐	☐
	(m) Past history of pension increases including details of any discretionary practices	☐	☐	☐	☐	☐
121	With respect to any defined benefit pension plan, furnish a copy of the most recently filed Form PBGC-1	☐	☐	☐	☐	☐
122	With respect to each pension plan that is a "multi-employer plan", furnish a statement of the employer's "withdrawal liability" within the meaning of ERISA 4211	☐	☐	☐	☐	☐

Ref	ITEM DESCRIPTION	Previously Provided	Provided With List	To be Provided	None	Not Applicable
Legal & Compliance Issues						
123	Provide details for the past three years to include date, charge and disposition for:	☐	☐	☐	☐	☐
	(a) EEOC charges	☐	☐	☐	☐	☐
	(b) Conciliation agreements	☐	☐	☐	☐	☐
	(c) OFCCP Audit findings	☐	☐	☐	☐	☐
	(d) Wrongful termination claims	☐	☐	☐	☐	☐
	(e) Wage and hour claims	☐	☐	☐	☐	☐
124	Pending lawsuits	☐	☐	☐	☐	☐
125	Copy of the Affirmative Action Plan (AAP), EE0-1, VETS-100	☐	☐	☐	☐	☐
Labor Relations						
126	Details of union status, copies of collective agreements/union contracts, grievance log, and any industrial relations problems over the last five years.	☐	☐	☐	☐	☐
127	Description and copies and current status of any pending or threatened arbitration, written grievance proceeding or labor dispute, description of bargaining history for the last three years negotiations, including unfair labor practice complaints, strikes, boycotts and picketing.	☐	☐	☐	☐	☐

Ref	ITEM DESCRIPTION	Previously Provided	Provided With List	To be Provided	None	Not Applicable
128	Copies of any correspondence/ communications with any union or employee body (*).	☐	☐	☐	☐	☐
Worker's Compensation						
129	Carrier - Insured or self-insured.	☐	☐	☐	☐	☐
130	Copy of accident log, OSHA log and any other record of health and safety issues for past three years.	☐	☐	☐	☐	☐
131	Details of current and historical workers compensation cost and any on-going, work-related claims.	☐	☐	☐	☐	☐
132	Details of workers compensation arrangements with third party providers and claims history (for the past 5 years) / provisioning levels.	☐	☐	☐	☐	☐
133	List any potential large claims.	☐	☐	☐	☐	☐
134	List of open workers compensation claims including date of injury, type of injury, current status, if out of service possible return date.	☐	☐	☐	☐	☐
Systems						
135	Timekeeping system	☐	☐	☐	☐	☐
136	Payroll	☐	☐	☐	☐	☐
137	HRIS	☐	☐	☐	☐	☐
138	Other HR, payroll or benefit systems	☐	☐	☐	☐	☐

Ref	ITEM DESCRIPTION	Previously Provided	Provided With List	To be Provided	None	Not Applicable
	Outside Consultants/Temporary Services/Outsourcing					
139	Details of all persons working for business not classified as an employee – provide copies of all consulting and management agreements	☐	☐	☐	☐	☐
	ENVIRONMENTAL					
140	Copies of any previous internal or external environmental audits and environmental impact statements that have been inferred or made in last 5 years, including Phase I, II and III reports	☐	☐	☐	☐	☐
141	Copies of any available information on the local sub-surface geological, hydro-geological and hydrological conditions in the immediate vicinity of the facilities	☐	☐	☐	☐	☐
142	Discharge consents for process waste water	☐	☐	☐	☐	☐
143	Plans indicating the location of above ground and underground storage vessels and tanks and their associated pipework including dates of installation, results of integrity testing, containment and appropriate certification	☐	☐	☐	☐	☐
144	List of all hazardous materials, inc asbestos, in structures or processes	☐	☐	☐	☐	☐
145	Air emission permits	☐	☐	☐	☐	☐
146	Citations from any statutory or regulatory bodies relating to any non-compliance issues	☐	☐	☐	☐	☐

Ref	ITEM DESCRIPTION	Previously Provided	Provided With List	To be Provided	None	Not Applicable
147	Information on contamination, emissions and spillage that have originated from of the activities of or that have occurred in connection with real properties, buildings or facilities which are or have been owned or used by the Company. Information on possible landfills, waste dumps or the equivalent which are or have been used by the Company or which are located on a real property owned or used by the Company	☐	☐	☐	☐	☐
148	Information on environmental sanction charges or company fines, which have been or can be expected to be imposed on the Company, claims for clean-up which have or can be raised against the Company as well as orders, injunctions or prohibitions by authorities, municipalities or the equivalent with respect to environmental and health issues	☐	☐	☐	☐	☐
149	Documentation with regard to clean-up measures that are planned or have been taken in connection with real properties which may have been affected by the activities of the Company or real properties, buildings or facilities which are or have been owned or used by the Company	☐	☐	☐	☐	☐

Ref	ITEM DESCRIPTION	Previously Provided	Provided With List	To be Provided	None	Not Applicable
150	Other correspondence, relating to the environment or health issues with authorities, municipalities or the equivalent regarding the activities of the Company or real properties, buildings or facilities which are or have been owned or used by the Company	☐	☐	☐	☐	☐
151	Claims or complaints from third parties such as neighbors, former employees or environmental organizations	☐	☐	☐	☐	☐
152	Information on environmental quality norms and classifications as environmental risk areas of real properties which are or have been owned or used by the Company	☐	☐	☐	☐	☐
153	A list of substances hazardous to the environment or human health, which are or have been used in the activities of the Company	☐	☐	☐	☐	☐
154	Permits from courts, authorities, municipalities or the equivalent regarding environmental or health issues, such as permits pursuant to the Environmental Act, the Environmental Code or water judgements.	☐	☐	☐	☐	☐
155	Notifications pursuant to the Environmental Code regarding the establishment or alteration of the activities of the Company	☐	☐	☐	☐	☐

Ref	ITEM DESCRIPTION	Previously Provided	Provided With List	To be Provided	None	Not Applicable
156	Applications for permits regarding environmental and health issues which have not yet been granted	☐	☐	☐	☐	☐
157	Information on the possible risk that obtained permits or the equivalent may be withdrawn, expire or be reconsidered or that provisions therein may be altered	☐	☐	☐	☐	☐
158	Environmental reports for the last three years and the supervisory authority's reply thereto	☐	☐	☐	☐	☐
159	Details for any environmental control program	☐	☐	☐	☐	☐
160	Information on possible violations of environmental and health regulations, permits or the equivalent or of conditions therein.	☐	☐	☐	☐	☐
161	Information with regard to the Company's handling of waste, such as the type and volume of waste deposited annually and information regarding how hazardous waste is handled.	☐	☐	☐	☐	☐
162	Agreements that contain possible outstanding environmental liabilities of the Company, such as environmental warranties, indemnities and other commitments made by the Company with regards to the environment, in, for example, rental agreements, leases, site leaseholds or in connection with the sale of business, real properties or site leaseholds.	☐	☐	☐	☐	☐

Ref	ITEM DESCRIPTION	Previously Provided	Provided With List	To be Provided	None	Not Applicable
163	Information on planned or decided alteration of the Company's activities or other circumstances which may lead to violations by the Company of laws, regulations or permits for its activities.	☐	☐	☐	☐	☐
164	Information on future circumstances that may affect The Company's activities from an environmental or health perspective, such as new legislation and regulations or any obligation to apply for permits or to file notifications with authorities or municipalities.	☐	☐	☐	☐	☐
PROPERTY						
165	Full description of all properties owned or occupied by the Company	☐	☐	☐	☐	☐
166	Copies of all leases, licenses, easements, sub-tenancy agreements and other matters affecting title to the land and buildings; furnish copies of deeds leases, sales contracts and appraisals	☐	☐	☐	☐	☐
167	Copies of any professional valuations of any property within the last three years	☐	☐	☐	☐	☐
168	Copies of title insurance policies or lawyers abstract reports covering the properties	☐	☐	☐	☐	☐
169	Describe all material zoning, building, environmental and similar laws, ordinances, and regulations to which the use of the properties referred to in 8.1 above is subject	☐	☐	☐	☐	☐

Ref	ITEM DESCRIPTION	Previously Provided	Provided With List	To be Provided	None	Not Applicable
170	Floor plans to scale of all buildings on the site plus elevational Plans of the "main" structures	☐	☐	☐	☐	☐
171	Details of the FBO in terms of:					
	(a) Existing Drawings	☐	☐	☐	☐	☐
	(b) Appraisals	☐	☐	☐	☐	☐
	(c) Certificate of Occupancy	☐	☐	☐	☐	☐
	(d) Safety Inspection Records	☐	☐	☐	☐	☐
	(e) Warranty Information (roofs, boilers, chillers, etc.)	☐	☐	☐	☐	☐
	(f) Records indicating age of material building systems (roof, paving, plumbing, heating, A/C, etc.)	☐	☐	☐	☐	☐
	(g) Historical cost incurred for repairs or improvements.	☐	☐	☐	☐	☐
	(h) Pending proposals for repairs or improvements.	☐	☐	☐	☐	☐
	(i) Description of future improvements planned.	☐	☐	☐	☐	☐
	(j) Outstanding citations for building and fire code violations.	☐	☐	☐	☐	☐
	(k) An ADA survey and status of any improvements implemented to effect physical compliance.	☐	☐	☐	☐	☐
	(l) Any previously prepared property condition assessment reports.	☐	☐	☐	☐	☐
	(m) Records of annual utility usage and cost. (Water, electric, gas, oil, etc.)	☐	☐	☐	☐	☐

Ref	Item Description	Previously Provided	Provided With List	To be Provided	None	Not Applicable
172	Details of any grants awarded for any buildings or Capital expenditures.	☐	☐	☐	☐	☐
173	Any abatement orders or building restrictions	☐	☐	☐	☐	☐
174	Current Net Book Value for each Freehold and Leasehold property location and the Basis of Valuation i.e. Open Market Value or Depreciated Replacement Cost or Historic Cost.	☐	☐	☐	☐	☐
TAX						
175	Copies of all tax returns (Federal and State), including amendments, and supporting/working schedules for last three years or longer if any previous periods remain open to audit.	☐	☐	☐	☐	☐
176	Copy of most recent Federal Revenue Agent Report (FRAR) or no change letter issued in connection with latest Federal Income Tax audit.	☐	☐	☐	☐	☐
177	Copies of information document requests notice of proposed adjustments and correspondence issued by the Internal Revenue Service or state taxing authorities regarding tax audits.	☐	☐	☐	☐	☐
178	Copy of most recent State Audit Report issued for states the company is registered to do business in or no change letter issued in connection with the latest State Income Tax audit.	☐	☐	☐	☐	☐

Ref	ITEM DESCRIPTION	Previously Provided	Provided With List	To be Provided	None	Not Applicable
179	Copies or explanation of any Federal or State statue that has been extended beyond the standard limitation period.	☐	☐	☐	☐	☐
180	Details of any correspondence/dispute with IRS/state tax authorities	☐	☐	☐	☐	☐
181	Details of any Federal/State tax examinations in progress	☐	☐	☐	☐	☐
182	Copies of any tax sharing arrangements, including any predecessors of the business (indemnities within sales contracts, etc.).	☐	☐	☐	☐	☐
183	Copies of all tax accrual work papers prepared for year-end purposes for the last three years, including analysis of reserve for tax contingencies.	☐	☐	☐	☐	☐
184	List of all tax accounting method changes made over the past three tax years, and the statutory authority for making such changes.	☐	☐	☐	☐	☐
185	Copy of analysis that details any Federal and State consolidated tax attributes attributable to the corporation (i.e.net operating losses, AMT credits, etc.)	☐	☐	☐	☐	☐
186	Copy of book, regular tax, alternative minimum tax and adjusted current earnings depreciation for the past three tax years. These reports should include asset basis, date placed in service, accumulated depreciation, depreciable life, and current year depreciation expense.	☐	☐	☐	☐	☐

Ref	ITEM DESCRIPTION	Previously Provided	Provided With List	To be Provided	None	Not Applicable
187	Copy of all transfer pricing agreements entered into with Federal or State taxing authorities.	☐	☐	☐	☐	☐
188	Provide details regarding transfer pricing methodologies.	☐	☐	☐	☐	☐
189	Copies of all agreements and general discussion of any intangibles that are licensed to others to use and the state where all licenses are located.	☐	☐	☐	☐	☐
190	Have any of the corporations been a party to a tax-free restructuring transaction? If so, please provide all related documents.	☐	☐	☐	☐	☐
191	Provide a list of any non-U.S. subsidiary, including:					
	Country of incorporation	☐	☐	☐	☐	☐
	(b) Description of business activities	☐	☐	☐	☐	☐
	Copies of all income and non-income tax filings during the past three years	☐	☐	☐	☐	☐
192	Copies of all analysis, matters, and disclosures regarding tax shelters for Federal and State tax returns.	☐	☐	☐	☐	☐
193	Copies of all tax opinions or memorandum received in the last three years.	☐	☐	☐	☐	☐
194	Copies related to the most recent customs audits.	☐	☐	☐	☐	☐
195	List of all states in which the company is registered or qualified to do business.	☐	☐	☐	☐	☐

Ref	ITEM DESCRIPTION	Previously Provided	Provided With List	To be Provided	None	Not Applicable
196	Please indicate the states in which the company has employees, independent contractors, agents or other representatives, and provide the following services: Authority to approve or accept orders, investigate the credit worthiness of customers, collect payments from customers, check customers inventory for reorders, pick up or replace damaged or returned property (if so, how often), provide training classes, seminars, or lectures to customers.	☐	☐	☐	☐	☐
197	List all states in which the company is currently remitting payroll taxes.	☐	☐	☐	☐	☐
Payroll Tax						
198	Copies of all Federal and State employment tax returns filed for the prior three years	☐	☐	☐	☐	☐
199	Copies of Forms 1099 filed with the Internal Revenue Service for the past three years	☐	☐	☐	☐	☐
Sales and Use Tax						
200	Copies of sales and use tax returns filed for the past three years or a list of states where sales and use tax returns have been filed and related expense	☐	☐	☐	☐	☐
201	Copies of the most recent sales and use tax audits for each jurisdiction.	☐	☐	☐	☐	☐

Ref	ITEM DESCRIPTION	Previously Provided	Provided With List	To be Provided	None	Not Applicable
202	Describe any outsourcing arrangements for sales and use tax purposes, including details as to the process for this arrangement.	☐	☐	☐	☐	☐
Property Tax						
203	List by jurisdiction of personal or real property owned by the corporation, which is located at a facility that is not owned by the corporation.	☐	☐	☐	☐	☐
204	Copies of all property tax returns (real and personal) filed for the past three years.	☐	☐	☐	☐	☐
205	Discussion of personal and real property tax abatements and assessments received from local tax authorities and the expiration date of the related agreements.	☐	☐	☐	☐	☐
206	Results and year of most recent personal property tax audit.	☐	☐	☐	☐	☐
207	Describe any outsourcing arrangements for property tax purposes, including details as to the process for this arrangement.	☐	☐	☐	☐	☐
Tax Administration						
208	Copies of schedules used to gather year-end tax information that reconciles into the financial statements.	☐	☐	☐	☐	☐
209	List of individuals who are responsible for providing year-end tax data?	☐	☐	☐	☐	☐
210	Who is primarily responsible for sales and use tax filings?	☐	☐	☐	☐	☐

Ref	ITEM DESCRIPTION	Previously Provided	Provided With List	To be Provided	None	Not Applicable
211	What software package is utilized to compute financial statement, tax, and alternative minimum tax, and adjusted current earnings depreciation? Where are those records maintained?	☐	☐	☐	☐	☐
OPERATIONS						
212	Copies of all supplier contracts/orders/ service agreements where annual purchases exceed $50,000 (*)	☐	☐	☐	☐	☐
213	Copy of operation procedures manual	☐	☐	☐	☐	☐
214	Copies and information on all Training Programs	☐	☐	☐	☐	☐
Financial						
215	Monthly financial statements, year-to-date previous 5 years	☐	☐	☐	☐	☐
216	Explanation of any unusual and extraordinary gains or losses in accounts	☐	☐	☐	☐	☐
217	Reconciliation of management accounts to audited financial statements	☐	☐	☐	☐	☐
218	Copy of the latest Strategic Plan / Business Plan	☐	☐	☐	☐	☐
219	Budgets/forecasts made over the last 3 years projecting forward 5 years including balance sheets, income statements and cash flows. Provide details of all main assumptions and identify key success factors. Explanation of major variances for 3 years to date actual versus budget	☐	☐	☐	☐	☐

Ref	ITEM DESCRIPTION	Previously Provided	Provided With List	To be Provided	None	Not Applicable
220	Detailed internal financial records (i.e. general ledger summary by major account)	☐	☐	☐	☐	☐
221	Copy of the accounting policy manual	☐	☐	☐	☐	☐
222	Details of any accounting policy changes	☐	☐	☐	☐	☐
223	Details of auditors and length of relationship. Access to auditor working papers (and accountants' management letters on internal controls and contingent liabilities for the past 5 years) is required	☐	☐	☐	☐	☐
224	Copies of any correspondence with external accountants relating to special consulting projects or disagreements over accounting issues	☐	☐	☐	☐	☐
225	Copies of any external auditors management letter or controls observation summary	☐	☐	☐	☐	☐
226	Name and branch address of all banks at which the Company has an account. Details of all financial details including inter alia, quoted and loan, debtors of credit, promissory note, guarantees and deposits, and cross guarantees structures, including all signatories for all accounts	☐	☐	☐	☐	☐
227	Lists and copies of all guarantees and indemnities.					
	(a) Given by the Company in relation to obligations of any other person and	☐	☐	☐	☐	☐

Ref	ITEM DESCRIPTION	Previously Provided	Provided With List	To be Provided	None	Not Applicable
	(b) Given by any other person in respect of the obligations of the Company	☐	☐	☐	☐	☐
NET ASSETS						
Fixed Assets						
228	Fixed asset register / listing showing full details including description of asset, cost, date of purchase, age, depreciated value, useful life, whether bought or leased	☐	☐	☐	☐	☐
229	Capex summary for last 3 years and forecast for next 5 years	☐	☐	☐	☐	☐
230	Existing capital commitments (Capex to be split as discretionary, repair or expansion)	☐	☐	☐	☐	☐
231	Details of any idle assets, assets fully written off or still in use or assets located off-site	☐	☐	☐	☐	☐
232	Details of any assets subject to a charge, mortgage, lien, encumbrance etc.	☐	☐	☐	☐	☐
233	Details of any assets used in the business which are not owned by the business	☐	☐	☐	☐	☐
234	Details of any grants, financial assistance etc, obtained in respect of any assets purchased	☐	☐	☐	☐	☐
235	Schedule of any long term investments	☐	☐	☐	☐	☐
Debt						
236	Analysis of debtors between accounts receivable and other debtors (including prepaid expenses, deferred charges etc)	☐	☐	☐	☐	☐

Ref	ITEM DESCRIPTION	Previously Provided	Provided With List	To be Provided	None	Not Applicable
237	Aged analysis of accounts receivable by customer/product	☐	☐	☐	☐	☐
238	Analysis of bad debt provision and movements	☐	☐	☐	☐	☐
239	Analysis of bad debt write-off by customer	☐	☐	☐	☐	☐
240	Details of credit terms granted, including expectations	☐	☐	☐	☐	☐
241	Schedule of other debtors	☐	☐	☐	☐	☐
242	Summary of all accounts in dispute or in process of legal collection	☐	☐	☐	☐	☐
243	Creditors	☐	☐	☐	☐	☐
244	Analysis of creditors between accounts payable and other creditors, accruals etc	☐	☐	☐	☐	☐
245	Aged analysis of accounts payable by supplier differentiating between trading payables and capital expenditure payables, reconciled to the general ledger	☐	☐	☐	☐	☐
246	Full details of accruals and other creditors including description of calculation methodology	☐	☐	☐	☐	☐
247	Analysis of all provisions and movements	☐	☐	☐	☐	☐
248	Description of cut-off policy for payables and expenses at month and year end and any changes over last 3 years	☐	☐	☐	☐	☐
249	Detail warranty policy, calculation of reserve and experience over last 3 years	☐	☐	☐	☐	☐

Ref	ITEM DESCRIPTION	Previously Provided	Provided With List	To be Provided	None	Not Applicable
	Inventory					
250	Details of accounting policy for raw material, bought in, WIP, finished goods and other inventory costing process and any changes over the last 3 years	☐	☐	☐	☐	☐
251	Policy regarding physical stock checks and details of any changes over last 3 years	☐	☐	☐	☐	☐
252	Stock listing showing aging	☐	☐	☐	☐	☐
253	Analysis of stock valuation by major product (fuel, raw material, WIP etc) showing gross valuation, obsolescence and net valuation, with reconciliation to general ledger	☐	☐	☐	☐	☐
254	Analysis of inventory reserve for obsolete, slow moving or other inventory issues	☐	☐	☐	☐	☐
255	Details of book – physical stock adjustments	☐	☐	☐	☐	☐
256	Details of any stock held on consignment or free issue stock or inventory held offsite or third party	☐	☐	☐	☐	☐
257	Schedule of inventory turnover rates by customer/product	☐	☐	☐	☐	☐
	Other					
258	Brief description of intercompany charges policy and all intercompany accounts and including the basis of transfer pricing (divisions, companies and subsidiaries	☐	☐	☐	☐	☐

Ref	ITEM DESCRIPTION	Previously Provided	Provided With List	To be Provided	None	Not Applicable
259	Details of all borrowings / financings including details of provider of finance, description of the nature of the financing, description of any security, amount outstanding, repayment terms	☐	☐	☐	☐	☐
260	Summary of major outstanding commitments, including fixed asset purchase, inventory purchases, advertising campaigns, plant construction, long term purchases and sales agreements, employment contracts and profit-sharing and similar plans	☐	☐	☐	☐	☐
261	Details of information on seasonal and mid-month variations in working capital	☐	☐	☐	☐	☐
	TRADING					
	Sales					
262	Sales (volumes and monetary amounts) and gross margin forecasts, by customer/product, for the next three years and details of background/ supporting information used to prepare sales volumes	☐	☐	☐	☐	☐
263	Schedule reconciling gross sales to net sales, detailing discounts, returns etc	☐	☐	☐	☐	☐
264	For FBOs:	☐	☐	☐	☐	☐
	(a) Gallons by type of fuel	☐	☐	☐	☐	☐
	(b) Gallons and margin by customer	☐	☐	☐	☐	☐
	(c) List of customer fuel discounts	☐	☐	☐	☐	☐
	(d) Average selling price by fuel type	☐	☐	☐	☐	☐

Ref	ITEM DESCRIPTION	Previously Provided	Provided With List	To be Provided	None	Not Applicable
	(e) Average cost of fuel	☐	☐	☐	☐	☐
	(f) Into-plane gallons by customer with pricing (per gallon or per flight)	☐	☐	☐	☐	☐
265	List of all hangar and tie-down tenants	☐	☐	☐	☐	☐
266	Volume and value of intercompany sales and purchases. Provide details of transfer pricing methodology and elimination of intercompany revenues and profits	☐	☐	☐	☐	☐
267	Details of any seasonal or cyclical sales patterns	☐	☐	☐	☐	☐
268	Details of current order book and back-log by customer/product and schedules of any contracts which are expected or have been loss making	☐	☐	☐	☐	☐
269	Details of significant related party transactions	☐	☐	☐	☐	☐
270	Policy on rebates, discounts etc	☐	☐	☐	☐	☐
271	Details of all customer warranties, indemnities or guarantees in existence	☐	☐	☐	☐	☐
	Information Technology					
	I.T.					
272	List of hardware and software used by the Company					
273	List any software licensing agreements					
274	List any Microsoft licenses by type and program					

Ref	ITEM DESCRIPTION	Previously Provided	Provided With List	To be Provided	None	Not Applicable
275	Listing of type of phone system, voice and fax lines, telephone equipment and services					
276	List all telephone numbers & cell numbers					
277	List the type of circuit, connectivity to buildings and airports,					
278	Description of network and phone cabling as well as ports available,					
279	List LAN line number and address (virtual or physical) for billing					
280	Provide contact person for installation of new circuit;					
281	Listing of any IT personnel, duties, function and number of employees used at each location;					
282	List IT suppliers and outsourced contracts;					
283	What systems are used for payroll and compensation?					

Glossary

Bill of Sale

A certificate of transfer of personal property. (Oxford Dictionary)

Discounted Cashflow Method (a valuation method)

A valuation method used to estimate the attractiveness of an investment opportunity. (Investopedia)

EBITDA

Earnings before interest, taxes, depreciation, and amortization.

Seller's Discretionary Earnings

The pre-tax earnings of the business before non-cash expenses, compensation, interest expense or income, as well as one-time and non-business related income and expense items. (ValuAdder)

Owner Benefit

Refers to the benefits an owner receives from his company/paid for by his company such as compensation, bonuses, health insurance premiums, life insurance premiums, auto allowances, cell phone allowances, personal meals, entertainment, travel, and so on.

Reps & Warranties

Reps and warranties is a term used to describe the assertions that a buyer and/or seller makes in a purchase and sale agreement. Both parties are relying on each other to provide a true account of all information and supporting documents to close the transaction.

The seller's representations usually relate to information that the buyer is relying on to value a company. Therefore, the seller attests to the truthfulness and accuracy of information delivered to the buyer. (Divestopedia)

Stock Sale

A stock sale is the purchase of the owner's shares of the business.

Asset Sale

The purchase of a company's assets without the transfer of ownership of the actual business entity. (**www.tuckerlaw.com** - Tucker/Arsenberg Attorneys: Asset vs. Stock Sales 101: The Very Basics)

Indemnities

Protection against financial loss.

Indemnifications

Protections against financial loss.

Environmental Phase I, Phase II

Phase I – An environmental assessment/detailed investigation into the history of the property and its former uses as it pertains to environmental risk of a buyer's investment. Phase I environmental assessments include a detailed onsite inspection of the property to identify hidden risks and/or non-compliance. (Wikipedia)

Phase II – Based on the findings of the Phase I, if a site is considered to possibly contain contamination, a Phase II environmental site assessment may be conducted and may include chemical analysis for hazardous substances. (Wikipedia)

SBA Loans (Small Business Administration)

U.S. government agency established to promote the economy by providing assistance to small businesses. (Investopedia)

Goodwill

The established reputation of a business regarded as a quantifiable asset and calculated as part of its value when sold. (Oxford Dictionary)

Liens

A lien is an encumbrance on one person's property to secure a debt the property owner owes to another person.

Non-compete

Legal term under which one party agrees not to enter into a similar profession in competition against another party. Usually within an employer-employee relationship.

UCC filings

Required filings under the Uniform Commercial Code.

Seller's notes/Promissory Note

A note in which one party promises to pay a sum to another party, under specific terms, for some consideration.

Rollover of Equity

The receipt of shares from the buyer as full or partial consideration for the purchase of a selling company. (Divestopedia)

Working Capital

The capital of a business which is used in its day-to-day trading operations, calculated as the current assets minus the current liabilities (Oxford Dictionary/Investopedia)

Working Capital Adjustment

At closing, if the actual working capital delivered is more or less than the working capital target, then usually a dollar for dollar adjustment upwards (if working capital is more than the peg) or downwards (if working capital is less than peg) occurs. (Divestopedia)

Working Capital Target

The desired working capital in order to run the day to day business operations

About the Author:

Emery Ellinger
Founder & CEO, Aberdeen
Advisors, Inc.

emery@aberdeenadvisors.com

727-639-4716

Before founding Aberdeen Advisors, Emery earned his business and financial expertise as a banker, corporate advisor and president of several companies. After receiving his Bachelor of Arts degree in Economics from Washington & Lee University, he rapidly rose through the ranks at Bank South and later Merrill Lynch, before becoming an entrepreneur.

He founded Aberdeen Marketing, Inc., a marketing company that he built from the ground up into a $7 million revenue and eventually sold to a larger firm. Emery has expertise in all areas of M&A Advisory practice. He has successfully completed hundreds of transactions, including mergers, acquisitions, divestitures and financings. His proven track record includes highly complex deals, including merging a traditional consulting business with an Internet company, then securing venture capital funding of $6 million. He also conceived and led the acquisition strategy of two companies, which resulted in the largest national source of government bids, valued at more than $1 billion. Emery is repeatedly recognized as a leading mergers and acquisitions executive in the Tampa Bay market and is well known throughout the South for his ability to connect ideal buyers with sellers. His primary industries of focus are healthcare, manufacturing, distribution and business services.

Emery is a strong believer in giving back to the community. He is an active member of Leadership Tampa Bay and serves on the Board of Directors of ACG, the St. Anthony's Hospital Foundation, and was previously on the State of Florida Board of Leasing. He enjoys golf and traveling in his spare time.

CPSIA information can be obtained
at www.ICGtesting.com
Printed in the USA
FFOW05n1042081017